BANFF'S BEST
DAYHIKES

BANFF'S BEST
DAYHIKES

BY
HEATHER ELTON

LONE
PINE

The Publisher: **Lone Pine Publishing**

#206, 10426-81 Avenue	#202A, 1110 Seymour Street	16149 Redmond Way, #180
Edmonton, AB	Vancouver, BC	Redmond, WA
Canada T6E 1X5	Canada V6B 3N3	USA 98052

Canadian Cataloguing in Publication Data
Elton, Heather, 1957–
    Banff's best dayhikes

    Includes index.
    ISBN 1-55105-093-5

    1. Banff National Park (Alta.)—Guidebooks. 2. Hiking—Alberta—Banff National Park—Guidebooks. 3. Trails—Alberta—Banff National Park—Guidebooks. I. Title.
GV199.44C22B42 1997   917.123'32   C97-910289-8

Senior Editor: Nancy Foulds
Editor: Lee Craig
Production Manager: David Dodge
Design: Heather Elton
Layout and Production: Federico Caceres, Gregory Brown, Carol S. Dragich
Cover Design: Federico Caceres
Photography: Heather Elton
Additional photography:
Harvey Locke: cover, 2, 26–27, 34, 40, 46–47, 50, 60, 90–91, 93.
David Dodge: 3, front and back cover insets.
Separations and Film: Elite Lithographers Co. Ltd., Edmonton, Alberta, Canada
Printing: Select Colour Press, Edmonton, Alberta, Canada
Illustrations: Gary Ross, Ian Sheldon
Many thanks for last minute assistance to Susan Sax and Janice Stolz.
The publisher gratefully acknowledges the support of Alberta Community Development and the Department of Canadian Heritage.

Contents

1. Banff's Best Dayhikes

2. Best Dayhikes near the Town of Banff

3. Best Dayhikes in the Town of Banff

Preface

The Canadian Rockies rock my world! When the golden light at dusk catches the glittering peaks around Banff, the beauty is so sublime that I understand the meaning of the Native American phrase, 'It's a good day to die.' I attribute this profound state of bliss to being unplugged from the technological world and tuned into the surrounding wilderness. Nature unblemished by human touch is the most perfect thing on the planet.

When walking in downtown Banff, it's hard to believe that a century ago it was a remote Canadian Pacific Railway (CPR) town, where Indians, outfitters, guides and prospectors eked out an existence, beyond the imagination of the rest of the world. Then came the famous railway poster campaigns promoting the spectacular scenery and enticing an emerging tourist class to experience the 'healing waters' at the hot springs. Since that time, Banff has turned into a chic international destination. Nowadays, people flock here for world-class shopping and visits to exclusive spas, and the likeliest place for tourists to spot an elk is while shopping on Banff Avenue. Fortunately, most people still come here for the phenomenal natural beauty.

However, with over five million tourists a year now visiting the park, increased human activity brings with it an impending crisis for the natural world. Parks Canada has a difficult task: to meet the demands of increased tourism, while preserving the surrounding wilderness. It's a juggling act that raises tough questions. How do we cope with increased visitation if no new facilities are built? Can we ensure ecological integrity as well as a sustainable economy? Although there is enormous pressure to sacrifice ecological integrity for short-term benefit, tourism, in the end, has to be based on a healthy environment. If wilderness isn't protected, we will lose the precious resource that brings visitors to the park in the first place.

The Canadian Rockies is one of the few places left where, for the most part, the order of the natural world prevails. The backcountry still looks much the same as it did for centuries when the land was laced together by Indian trails. Some of the hikes described in this book are the very same routes. They take you to places of pristine beauty, to some of the world's most fragile ecosystems. As you walk along them, take the opportunity to go within yourself and listen to your heart. Respect the land. By hiking with care and leaving no trace of your passing in the landscape, you will protect the earth's wildness for generations to come.

This book is dedicated to the Canadian Rockies and the many people with whom I have shared the experience of moving through that landscape, especially Kevin Brooker, Gordon Ferguson, Anne Georg, Mary Beth Laviolette, Douglas MacLean, Jak Oliver, Sverre Reid, Don Romanchuk, Ricardo Velasquez and Robin Yager. I am especially grateful to my parents who introduced me to the mountains before I could walk and took me camping each summer of my youth. I also want to acknowledge Mr. and Mrs. H.W. Klassen and their daughter Lynn, who took me to Lake O'Hara at the age of 13. It was in this pristine environment that I was first inspired by the beauty of nature and learned to travel through the various mountain terrains with confidence. I am eternally grateful to Kevin Brooker who rekindled my passion to ski after a decade hiatus. I owe a special thanks to my telemarking pals who have toured with me into the backcountry and given me further insight into the mountain landscape. I am thankful for all of these experiences, because they have given me a deep appreciation and respect for wilderness.

Disclaimer

When hiking in Banff National Park, there are many potential dangers you could face: aggressive wildlife, bad weather, difficult trails, floods, mud slides, rock falls, forest fires, avalanches and snow lingering long after hiking season begins.

The author has done her best to explain the conditions, trail information and potential hazards involved when hiking in the Banff area. It is important to remember that these conditions can, and do, change, and that every person has his or her limits. The individual hiker has to be the judge of his or her own physical condition and level of hiking skill. However, even the most advanced hiker has to realize that nothing is guaranteed—carelessness, rapidly changing weather, 'Acts of God' or just plain 'bad luck' can all have deadly consequences.

The author and publisher cannot be held responsible for any thefts, problems, injuries or misfortunes that occur from use of the material in this book.

With this caution in mind, best wishes for enjoyable and safe hiking in Banff National Park!

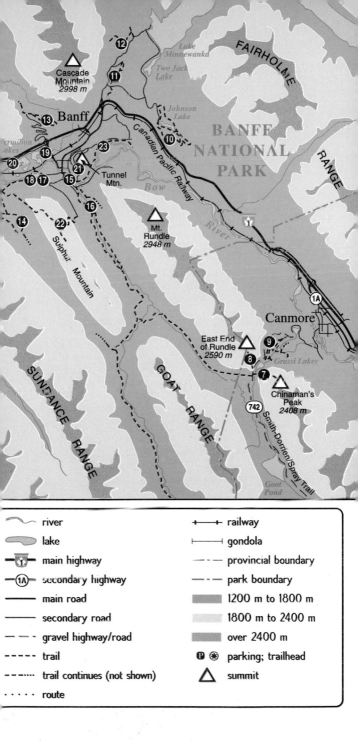

river
lake
main highway
(1A) secondary highway
main road
secondary road
gravel highway/road
trail
trail continues (not shown)
route

+—+ railway
|—| gondola
—··— provincial boundary
—·—· park boundary
1200 m to 1800 m
1800 m to 2400 m
over 2400 m
🅟 ✳ parking; trailhead
△ summit

Introduction

What makes this book different from other hiking books about the Canadian Rockies is its smaller size and focus on hikes specific to the Banff area. For years, I have photocopied the hike of the day to avoid lugging around a 300-page book, so I thought why not design a hiking book that could easily be stuffed into a pocket or backpack? *Banff's Best Dayhikes* focuses on trails within the Banff townsite and in the immediate vicinity—the furthest being Mt. Bourgeau, 20 minutes to the west, and Chinaman's Peak, 40 minutes to the east, near the town of Canmore.

The hikes are representative of the surrounding Banff landscape, and are, therefore, varied both in terrain and difficulty. Obviously, it is impossible to include all the hikes in the area in a book this size. You only have to look in any direction to see that there is unlimited backcountry adventure. I have had the pleasure of hiking all the trails in this book, and have chosen a mix of easy front-country hikes and more challenging backcountry ones.

If you hike all of these trails, you will travel through the montane valley into subalpine and alpine ecoregions. Trails wind though forests of white spruce, lodgepole pine, Douglas fir, Lyall's larch and aspen. Some trails lead into the world's largest alpine meadow system—fields dotted with glacial tarns and a profusion of colourful wildflowers in mid-summer. Some paths take you by rushing creeks, past cascading waterfalls to azure lakes, through windy mountain passes and up steep talus slopes to precipitous peaks. Believe it or not, many paths travel through wetlands to visit bog life. Other trails have geological and historical significance. All the trails lead to beautiful places with spectacular views. There is a hike for everyone in this book. Determine whether you want to do a full-day or half-day hike, know your endurance level, read the hike description, take extra food and clothing, and have an excellent day on the perfect hike.

There are easy nature walks with minimal elevation gain, strenuous full-day hikes for seasoned hikers and easy scrambles. Fit pedestrians who are content to walk on a paved path to Sundance Canyon, Bow River Hoodoos or along Johnson Lake should probably not attempt to scramble the East End of Rundle, climb Cory Pass, or do the mega-circuit route

Banff National Park's birthplace is the hot springs at the Cave & Basin. Legend has it that two American prospectors—one of them John Healy of Healy Pass fame—stumbled upon the springs in 1874 following directions from Stoney Natives whose tribe had used the warm waters for centuries. Healy intended to stake a claim on the springs, but lacked the financial resources to hire a surveyor. The springs faded back into obscurity until 1883, when three Canadian Pacific Railway (CPR) workers—Tom and William McCardell and Frank McCabe—stumbled upon the cave when they were prospecting for minerals on Sulphur Mountain.

Apparently, the men used a tree as a ladder to lower themselves into the cave, where, through the mist below, they discovered the sulfurous waters. Because a hot bath was such a luxury in those days, the three envisioned fabulous wealth and built a shack to establish their claim. But because Banff had yet to be surveyed and the Canadian government did not recognize hot water as a mineral on which to base a claim, no lease was granted. By this time, the hot springs had become local knowledge and others attempted to file claims thinking the site was a licence to print money.

Unknown to any of the prospectors, the CPR management, recognizing that the spectacular scenery would attract tourists and promote the railway, had already proposed that a federal reserve be established in Banff. The government approved the 26-sq. km (10-sq. mi) Banff Hot Springs Reservation on November 28, 1885—Canada's first national park and the world's third, after Yellowstone National Park, U.S., and Royal National Park, Australia.

In 1887 a further expansion of land formed Rocky Mountain Parks Reserve, which was renamed Banff National Park in 1930.

from Healy Pass to Sunshine Meadows. Before you scramble up from Harvey Pass to the peak of Mt. Bourgeau, build your skill and endurance level by doing less challenging hikes first—like Tunnel or Sulphur mountain.

Rating the Hikes

What is difficult for one person may be easy for another. The hikes in this book are rated as easy, moderate and difficult. **Easy** trails and nature walks can be hiked by most fit people; some are

Overview of Banff townsite.

on paved paths and are wheelchair accessible.

Moderate trails have gradual elevation gain and can be completed in six hours.

Difficult refers to hikes with intense elevation gain, or hikes that are several hours long and require endurance and possibly minor technical skills, like negotiating scree and boulder fields. The three scrambles included in the book—East End of Rundle, Chinaman's Peak and Mt. Bourgeau—are 'easy' scrambles in that they don't require technical climbing gear and most of the routes can be done upright rather than hav-ing to use your hands. However, they are difficult hikes because of the significant elevation gain, occasional cliff bands, scree slopes and mild exposure. Unless you are compelled to conquer a mountain peak, you probably should do a hike rather than a scramble. Scrambles are for the experienced hiker who wants to be challenged. Less experienced hikers should keep this caution in mind.

The Trails

With the exception of ridge walks or scrambles along obscure trails through scree slopes, most of the hikes in this book are on well-graded trails. There is a mixture of established pack trails, game trails, fire or logging roads, pine-needle paths and asphalt trails. Expect to find parking lots and outhouses at trailheads. Junctions on official trails in Banff National Park are marked by yellow and brown hiking signs. Cairns and paint splotches on boulders indicate the route above treeline.

Because everyone moves at a different speed, the time it takes to complete a hike is estimated for the average hiker. 'Ascent time' refers to how long it takes to get from the trailhead to the destination—a one-way calculation unless specified as a circuit or loop trail. Half-day hikes usually take four hours return; dayhikes take six hours; and full-day hikes take up to 10 hours. Those hikers stopping to investigate wildflowers may find that it takes longer than indicated, and seasoned hikers may find it takes less time to reach their destination.

Read the hike descriptions carefully to determine which hike is best for you, depending on whether you want a relaxing hike with lunch beside a mountain lake or an epic nine-hour peak 'assault.' Know your limits. If you are out of your depth, or just having a bad day, turn around and do something else.

Words of Caution

In comparison with the tropics, the Canadian Rockies have relatively few hazards. There are no poisonous snakes, spiders or insects, but the Rocky Mountain wood tick can cause Rocky Mountain spotted fever. Most of the hazards are naturally occurring: rough trails, fallen trees, mud, avalanches, swollen, unbridged rivers, contaminated drinking water, aggressive wildlife or extreme weather. If you take precautions to avoid a bear encounter and have brought extra clothes to stay warm in a hailstorm or blizzard, an infestation of persistent horseflies is usually as bad as it gets. In the following pages are a few words of advice to help you deal with potential hazards.

Drinking Water

Although the water looks refreshing in clear mountain streams, it is often infected with the *Giardi lamblia* parasite, which can cause severe gastrointestinal pain. The parasite is transmitted through animal fecal matter that ends up in streams. Water at high elevations or near the headwaters of a glacier can be safe, but you will be taking a risk. Always take your own water on a hike—there may be none available, or it may be infected.

Vermilion Lakes.

Bugs

Ticks are the most dangerous insect in the Canadian Rockies, because they sometimes carry Rocky Mountain spotted fever, which can cause paralysis or nervous disorders. Ticks hide in the tall grass of subalpine meadows, where they leap onto unsuspecting passing mammals, such as humans, to suck blood. Check yourself for ticks, especially on the neck and hairline, after a hike. If a tick embeds its mouth in your skin, remove it with a slow, steady pull, taking care not to dislodge its head. Another technique is to burn its body with a burnt but still hot match head. If you experience numbness or headaches from a possible tick bite, see a doctor. Insect repellents containing DEET help to protect you from ticks and mosquitoes.

Aggressive Wildlife

With increased human activity in the montane valley, there is an alarming increase in the number of people injured or attacked by aggressive wildlife, especially elk. Large herds of elk now live in the Banff townsite. The cows are the most dangerous during the calving season in May and June. Bull elk are aggressive during fall rut. These animals can cause serious bodily harm by pummeling you with their sharp hooves and antlers. Watch for them among the trees. If you do see some elk, avoid them. Never get between a mother and her calf or a bull elk and a female. Don't feed them. Don't park your vehicle too close to them. Please don't take your small child up to them for a photograph.

The well-graded trail to Bourgeau Lake passes through a montane valley.

If elk exhibit hostile behaviour, like a raised head, flattened-back ears, curled lips or swinging antlers, you are in danger! Use a jacket or another object to make yourself look bigger. An umbrella is perfect, if you have one with you. Protect yourself by moving into a thicket of trees too narrow for them to move through, climb a tree, or find a large tree or boulder to put between yourself and the animal. Never turn your back on an elk!

Bears are the other dangerous animals you could encounter. Usually, they'll avoid you, but a few now used to eating garbage at campsites have become more accustomed to humans. They are bolder than other bears. The number one rule is to do everything you can to avoid a bear encounter. Travel in groups. Make noise; sing and yell. Leave your dog at home. Watch for signs of bear scat, tracks or dug-up earth, and if you see any, leave the area.

If you spot a bear in the distance, leave as unobtrusively as possible. If you encounter one of these unpredictable wild creatures, avoid eye contact, speak in a soothing, non-threatening voice, and back away gently.

Whatever you do, don't run. Don't act like bait. Don't

By 1887 development in what was then called Banff Hot Springs Reservation was already well under way. A tunnel to the cave was blasted and bathhouses were installed. CPR medical supervisor, R.G. Brett, opened a private hospital/spa—the Brett Sanitarium—that attracted tourists from as far away as Europe on the promise that the hot springs would cure all ailments.

Brett built another healing centre, the Grand View Villa at the Upper Hot Springs, which may have been a front for a pool hall/massage parlour that sold iced beverages. There were many testimonials proclaiming the miraculous 'healing' powers of the water; the handrails of the staircase were even reinforced with discarded crutches from healed patients. (It later turned out that Brett prescribed crutches to all patients whether they needed them or not.) When the villa burned in 1901, the federal government cancelled Brett's lease and the development of the public facility began at the Upper Hot Springs. In 1914 the largest swimming pool in Canada was constructed. The growing number of visitors who flocked to the springs to satisfy the current fascination with 'healing waters' made these facilities necessary.

turn your back on a bear. If a bear charges, drop something to distract the bear. It may pause to investigate, giving you more time to get away. You could climb a tree, although bears are agile tree climbers. If attacked by a grizzly, curl up to protect your head, and play dead. If attacked by a black or brown bear, fight back. Many hikers carry a can of bear spray for protection, but you have to be very close to the bear for it to be effective.

None of the other large carnivores such as wolves, cougars or wolverines present a serious threat to your safety.

Weather

Weather changes fast in the Canadian Rockies. A perfect summer day can end in a blizzard. Sleet, snow, rain, cloud, sun, fog, mist and wind are all possible in a single day. Be prepared, or you could end up hypothermic and in big trouble. Extra clothes will save the day. Expect chilly and stormy weather in high altitudes; temperature decreases and precipitation increases with altitude.

Grizzly Bear

Typically, the hiking season extends from late May to early October in the lower altitudes, and from late June through mid-September at higher elevations. The average annual temperature at treeline is -4° C (25° F). Fall weather is characterized by cool, sunny days with colourful larches and no bugs. Midsummer evenings are long with twilight lasting until 10 p.m. (Banff weather report: 403–762–2088.)

Hypothermia

Cold air, precipitation and wind all contribute to hypothermia, a condition that lowers the core body temperature. Even a chilly wind on a summer day can put some hikers over the edge. Symptoms include shivering, cold hands and feet, and a lowering of the heartbeat and respiration. Because heat escapes through the head, it is advisable to wear a hat. If you have any of these symptoms, put on extra clothes and have a hot drink. If the condition progresses, extreme shivering may cause muscular rigidity, which results in stumbling and a loss of technical precision when hiking. Without expert medical attention, hypothermia can lead to unconsciousness and often death.

What to Wear

In the Canadian Rockies, weather can change faster than you can change your clothes. The most practical way to dress is in layers, so you can remove clothes if you get too warm, or put more on if you get chilled. Usually I begin a strenuous hike in shorts, a sleeveless T-shirt and a hat. In my pack are lightweight fleece stretch pants and a long-sleeved top, fleece jacket, nylon windbreaker, down vest, extra socks, bandanna, gloves and a winter hat. Rain gear is also a good idea on a full-day hike in alpine terrain. If you don't have a full rain suit, a heavy duty plastic garbage bag with a hole cut out for your head makes a decent waterproof poncho. Obviously, there are variations on any wardrobe. I prefer high-tech light-weight fabrics that dry quickly, rather than cotton or wool, which gets damp and is heavier. Whatever your preference, the important thing is to take with you enough clothing to keep warm in all con-ditions.

Synthetic hiking boots or sturdy hightop runners are all that are really required for the hikes listed in this book. Street shoes are okay for most of the short nature walks, certainly the ones on a paved path. However, it's hard to beat a lightweight leather hik-ing boot with sturdy rubber soles for comfort and support. They are more durable when negotiating scree, and provide more support when descend-ing trails. They are also water-proof.

What to Bring

Food is essential on a hike. In addition to your lunch, bring fruit and high protein trail snacks like nuts, choco-late or power bars for an energy boost. Although there can be an abundance of fresh water, it is not always safe to drink. In fact, mountain water rarely is safe with the possible exception of glacial rivulets at the headwaters of a glacier. Whether you want to take your chances with *Giardia* or

Short tailed Weasel

not, always carry water, because water does not exist on many of the hikes in this book. Portable, ceramic water filters are an effective screen for *Giardi lamblia,* and will ensure a ready supply of drinkable water on trails with water sources available.

Looking west towards the 'muleshoe' in the Bow River.

Other essentials include the following supplies: a pocket knife, toilet paper, UV sunglasses, waterproof matches, cigarette lighter, insect repellent, pen and paper, compass and a topographical map for the area you're exploring. This book provides topographical maps for the nine main hikes. A head-lamp or small flashlight can be useful if you should get caught outside after dark. Bring a first-aid kit with blister treatment, including bandages and moleskin, adhesive dressings, sterile gauze, tape, butterfly clips, tweezers, pain killers, tensor bandage and duct tape. Bear spray is also becoming increasing popular. Rubber boots and insect repellent are essential for exploration in the Fenland, marsh and wetlands areas.

Where to Tread

This book is dedicated to preserving the mountain environment. Please take exceptional care to leave the wilderness exactly as you find it. Here are a few trail etiquette rules to help you hike with minimal impact on the environment:

• Stay on the trails to avoid getting lost, getting in trouble on hazardous terrain, or damaging the fragile vegetation. Do not make shortcuts on switchbacks. Don't step off the trail to avoid muddy sections, even if doing so means muddy hiking boots. Stay off trails that are closed for rehabilitation. The alpine ecosystem is one of the most fragile in the world, and it takes decades for the vegetation to recover. If you must go off trail, tread lightly.

It is impossible to share all of Banff's secrets. There are limitless possibilities for backcountry adventure in all directions, and for those visitors who prefer to stay in the front country, the options are numerous as well. Take a golf lesson with a CPGA professional on the spectacular Banff Springs Hotel course, fly-fish the Bow River, canoe Forty Mile Creek and Vermilion Lakes, boat cruise Lake Minnewanka, river raft the Bow River, take an overnight trail ride, gondola up Sulphur Mountain, heli-picnic in the alpine meadows on Mt. Lady Macdonald, attend a theatre event during the Banff Arts Festival, visit the Whyte Museum of the Canadian Rockies, or shop along Banff Avenue. For total relaxation, soak in the Upper Hot Springs, or have an aromatherapy mineral bath or seaweed wrap at the luxurious Solace Spa at the Banff Springs Hotel.

• Don't feed the animals! They are wild. Really. They can kill you, especially the bears and elk. (If that doesn't deter you, perhaps the fact that it is illegal to feed wildlife—an offence under the National Parks Act—will.)

• It is illegal to remove any natural objects such as rocks, plants, flowers, antlers, etcera from Banff National Park. Never pick wild flowers or edible plants.

• Don't litter. Pack out all your garbage. Under no circumstances should you throw it in an outhouse. Don't leave cigarette butts on the trail—they take between one to five years to decompose.

• Use the public outhouse at the trailhead, or read Kathleen Meyer's book *How To Shit in the Woods*. If you have to go, choose a spot away from the trail or any streams, dig a hole, and when finished cover your excrement with earth, and restore the spot close to its original appearance. Human waste is a major factor in spreading *Giardi lamblia* in North America.

• Vehicles stopping in Banff National Park require a permit available from the Banff National Park entrance gate or an information centre. Bicycles are permitted only on designated trails.

• Leave your dog at home. It might disturb wildlife, other hikers and spread *Giardia lamblia*. Dogs have been

The establishment in 1885 of Banff Hot Springs Reservation, which was later called Banff National Park, set the precedent that the hot springs and the surrounding wilderness would belong to all Canadians and not to private interest. The *National Parks Act* (1930) declares, 'The parks are hereby dedicated to the people of Canada for their benefit, education and enjoyment ... and such places shall be maintained and made use of so as to remain unimpaired for future generations.'

known to incite grizzly attacks. If you must bring them, park regulations require that they be on a leash.

• Hunting and trapping of wildlife is not permitted.

• Women who are menstruating should be aware that bears may be attracted by the blood's odour. To minimize the risk of attracting a bear, wear a tampon, and take zip lock plastic bags to dispose of your used menstrual products.

• Respect the desire of others for solitude and quiet.

• The people hiking downhill have the right of way.

• Be prepared because help is seldom nearby. Take extra clothes and food. Many of these hikes go into wilderness where there are no amenities. Be responsible for your own safety. It is recommended that you don't travel alone—there really is safety in numbers. If you do go out alone, let someone know where you are going and when you expect to return.

Finally, your comments about this book are appreciated. As seasons change, so does the natural world. If you discover errors, please let us know. We strive to produce an accurate and reliable hiking book. Happy trails!

In an emergency contact

Banff RCMP (403) 762-2226
Banff Warden (403) 762-4506
Canmore RCMP (403) 678-5516
Canmore Emergency Services (emergency line)
    678-6199 (0) 591-7767

Pika tracks

White mountain avens on a rocky slope.

Telephone Numbers

Parks Canada (403) 292-4401

Banff Information Centre
   (403) 762 1550

Travel Alberta (800) 222-6501

Banff Weather (403) 762-2088

Road Report (403) 762-1450

Cave & Basin (403) 762-1566

Upper Hot Springs
   (403) 762-1515

Government of Alberta R.I.T.E.
line: Dial 310-0000 and ask the
operator to connect you to a government number free of charge.

Dark-eyed Junco

Originally called 'Siding 29,' the town of Banff was renamed in 1883 by William Cornelius Van Horne to honour the two largest stockholders of the Canadian Pacific Railway, Lord Strathcona (Donald Smith) and his cousin George Stephen. Banffshire, Scotland was Strathcona's hometown.

1
Banff's Best
Dayhikes

Harvey Lake is located in an alpine basin above Bourgeau Lake.

1-Bourgeau Lake
Difficulty: Easy
Distance: 7.5 km (4.7 mi)
Ascent Time: 2.5—4 hrs
Elevation Gain: 710 m (2328 ft)
Elevation: 2155 m (7068 ft)

Harvey Pass
Difficulty: Moderate
Distance: 9.7 km (6 mi)
Ascent Time: 3.5—5 hrs
Elevation Gain: 1035 m (3394 ft)
Elevation: 2450 m (8036 ft)

Bourgeau Peak

Difficulty: Easy scramble
Distance: 10.2 km (6.4 mi)
Ascent Time: 4–6 hours
Elevation Gain: 1500 m (4920 ft)
Elevation: 2930 m (9613 ft)
Topo Map: 82 O/4 Banff (trail not as marked)

Access: The Bourgeau Lake parking lot is on the S.W. side of the TransCanada Highway, 11.8 km (7.3 mi) west of Banff or 17.8 km (11 mi) east of Castle Junction. There is a highway sign signalling the parking lot's location for eastbound travellers only. The trailhead is behind the washrooms on the west side of the parking lot.

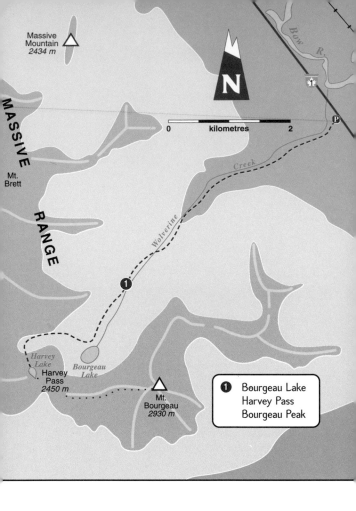

Many hikers consider Harvey Pass to be one of the most beautiful destinations in the Banff area. Its easy access from the townsite and gradual elevation gain also make it one of the most popular. This trail offers many options for hikers, enough to satisfy all levels of performance whether you want an easy dayhike looking at wildflowers or an intense nine-hour peak 'assault' via Mt. Bourgeau's west ridge. Enroute, hikers pass through three different ecoregions—montane, subalpine, alpine—each with something special to offer: rivers, waterfalls, lakes, glacial tarns, alpine meadows and a mountain pass with impressive panoramic views. Hikers can either picnic at Bourgeau Lake, climb the steep talus slopes to Harvey Pass, or

The cirque and scramble above Bourgeau Lake.

scramble up Mt. Bourgeau. Any way you do it, it's a full day.

The trail to Bourgeau Lake is submerged in a lodgepole pine and Douglas fir forest on the slopes of Wolverine Creek. The 710-m (2328-ft) elevation gain is distributed gradually along a well-trodden path that climbs steadily for 2.5 hours through some of the most lush vegetation in the Canadian Rockies.

In July there are numerous species of fungi and lichens growing on the path, as well as late-blooming orchids, prickly roses, wild strawberries, Indian paintbrushes, yellow and blue columbines, lavender harebells, purple clematis, pink fireweed and white yarrow, to name a few. Further in the forest are miniature lacy mitrewort, which are hidden from view in a car-

Harvey Pass was named by Jim Brewster after his cousin Ralph Harvey, who accompanied him to the pass in the 1920s while scouting terrain for a ski hill. In 1936, Brewster acquired Sunshine Village.

Purple saxifrage can be found growing on rocks.

pet of feather mosses, clubmosses and lichens. Other shade-loving plants, such as delicate twinflowers, fairy bells, bronze bells, bunchberries, kinnikinnik and wintergreens, grow beneath the dense spruce and fir canopy. Middens, or mounds of discarded seed shells from Englemann spruce cones, are evidence of red squirrels.

The trail continues upwards, while Wolverine Creek plummets into the gorge below. There are some beautiful glimpses of the vertical rock ridges and serrated peaks of the 350-million-year-old Sawback Range, aptly named in 1858 by Sir James Hector, a geologist. The path crosses a log bridge over a major tributary of Wolverine Creek at 3.7 km (2.3 mi). Because the waterfall, which cascades down from Lake Bourgeau above, is further ahead at 5.5 km (3.4 mi), the log bridge is a good spot for a rest. There is a profusion of cow parsnip, wild vetch, Solomon's seal, mountain sorrel, locoweed and fireweed around. Numerous shrubs of buffaloberry, wild gooseberry, Saskatoon berry, red osier dogwood and the interesting bracted honeysuckle line the path. This spot is an excellent location to soak feet, replenish liquids, and gather strength for the steep switchbacks up to the cirque. Mt. Brett dominates the landscape ahead.

Mt. Brett, Massive Range.

Part way up this steep section, we stepped aside—mostly out of trail etiquette but also out of surprise—to allow a pack of elderly hikers dressed in netted bug suits to pass. On this August day the horseflies were so evil that one landed every five seconds and ruined any possibility of a picnic in the alpine meadows. The horseflies are not necessarily so bad in June or July, but keep in mind, you take your chances.

Eventually, the trail levels out into a subalpine wet meadow before arriving at the cold, turquoise waters of Bourgeau Lake at 7.5 km (4.7 mi) from the trailhead. Situated within an amphitheatre carved into the limestone walls of Mt. Bourgeau, the lake is an attractive site for a picnic. There is plenty of terrain to wander, and in high summer the wildflowers are magnificent. The meadows are dotted with daisies, violets, larkspur, lousewort, bluebells, Indian paintbrushes, valerian, ragwort, aster, woolly everlastings, wild vetch and forget-me-nots. Look carefully, and you might see white-tailed ptarmigan in the piles of broken rock on the steep and barren talus slopes that flank Bourgeau Lake. Its high elevation—2155 m (7068 ft)—means that remnants of deep snow often linger well into summer.

 Mt. Bourgeau was first climbed in 1890 by pioneer J.J. McArthur and outfitter Tom Wilson. The mountain stands at 2930 m (9613 ft) high, and it takes approximately 4–6 hours to reach the peak from the trailhead.

Least Chipmunk

For strong hikers the one-hour, strenuous climb to Harvey Pass from Bourgeau Lake is well worth the effort. It is a 2.4-km (1.4-mi) hike with 295 m (968 ft) in elevation gain. Take any of several paths along the northwest lakeshore, through a stunted forest of subalpine fir and Lyall's larch, and begin the ascent up the steep hillside towards the notch between Mt. Bourgeau and Mt. Brett, the two most commanding peaks of the Massive Range. The rough path on the north side of the inlet stream takes you past a waterfall that links Bourgeau Lake to the small lake in the high alpine basin above. There are some great views of Bourgeau Lake, whose emerald hues intensify with altitude. The narrow path carves around bent 'wind timber,' or krummholz, signalling the treeline and upper limits of the subalpine ecoregion.

The high alpine basin is a magical place situated in the glacially carved cirque of Mt. Brett. In mid-summer the gentle landscape looks like a lime-green pincushion dotted with hardy dwarf perennials and brilliantly coloured alpine flowers. Nestled in the dense turf and woody mat-growing shrubs of alpine willow and juniper are moss campion, mountain heather, alpine buttercup, western anemone and glacier lily. Small waterfalls, rushing brooks and tundra

A tarn is a small, glacially formed lake with no surface outlet. Meltwater from cirque and other glaciers collects in bedrock depressions or behind moraines that were deposited by the receding glacier ice. The water escapes through cracks in the bedrock. There are three tarns above Bourgeau Lake, including Harvey Lake at Harvey Pass.

A glacial tarn is a lake without a surface outlet.

ponds make the basin sound especially lyrical. There are even three exquisite glacial tarns: unique mountain lakes without a surface outlet. It is the perfect terrain for golden-mantled ground squirrels, least chipmunks, weasels, martens, pikas and marmots.

Hikers will want to continue up the compacted scree trail for the final 15-minute slog to the exceptionally sce-nic Harvey Pass at 2450 m (8036 ft). Nestled in the hollow of Harvey Pass is the azure Harvey Lake, a perfect glacial tarn, which reflects superb views of Sunshine Meadows, Healy Creek, Simpson Pass, the Monarch Ramparts and Mt. Assiniboine. If you are lucky, you will see mountain goats and bighorn sheep. If you're not so lucky, a grizzly might see you.

For those hardy souls able to endure a nine-hour day, it is only another 450 m (1476 ft) to the peak of Mt. Bourgeau. The path to the summit follows the gentle west ridge, and goes up the exposed back shoulder. While the ascent is steep, the path is more of a hike for the two-legged than a scramble with hands and feet. There is hardly any loose scree, and other than an occasional boulder field the route is a pleasant walk. The scree path skirts snow cornices and dramatic ridges with spectacular views of Bourgeau Lake nestled in the cirque far below. Delicate alpine blossoms of purple saxifrage, golden fleabane, Lyall's rock cress, yellow and white mountain avens and stonecrop cling to the scree, seeking protection from the ever-present wind. The winter winds howl across this slope, dumping snow on the leeward side and leaving

Red paintbrushes with purple asters behind.

Hoary Marmot

these plants exposed. They protect themselves by growing low to the ground in dense mats, small rosettes or round cushions. It is astounding that anything grows on this wind-scoured slope, one of the most fragile ecosystems on the planet.

A man-made telecommunications tower at the summit shatters any solitude-in-the-wilderness theme, but if you turn your back to it you are surrounded by an ocean of mountain peaks. Mt. Brett, the Sawback Range and Mt. Assiniboine are all within view. The broad summit plateau and gentle ridge lines provide ample space to wander. Coarse shale shatters beneath your boots, making for a thrilling and speedy descent, not unlike telemark skiing.

Bourgeau Lake and Peak were named by James Hector, the Scotsman who was surgeon and geologist to the Palliser Expedition, in honour of Eugène Bourgeau. Bourgeau was a popular and highly esteemed French botanist who was the plant collector on the Palliser Expedition, which brought him to the Canadian Rockies from 1857–60. He collected 1200 plant species from western Canada. The Palliser Expedition, which was scientific in nature, travelled from the Red River Colony to and through the Rocky Mountains.

From Healy Pass looking towards Mt. Assiniboine.

2-Healy Pass

Difficulty: Moderate; some
steep sections
Distance: 9.2 km (5.7 mi)
Ascent Time: 3–4 hours
Elevation Gain: 700 m (2296 ft)
Elevation: 2330 m (7642 ft)
Topo Map: Banff 82 O/4

Access: Follow the TransCanada
Highway west of Banff for
8.3 km (5.2 mi) to the Sunshine
Village ski resort exit. Follow the
road from the exit for 9 km
(5.6 mi) to its end at the
gondola parking lot. The
trailhead is located in the S.W.
corner of the ski area parking
lot behind the lower gondola
terminal. (Don't take the
Sunshine Village access road.)

Healy Pass, Simpson Pass and the Sunshine Meadows are part of an extensive alpine meadow system connected by a trail that meanders through the various passes along the eastern edge of the Great Divide. The rolling meadows span a 15-kilometre (9.3-mi) arc, from Citadel Pass to the Monarch Ramparts. Wildflowers bloom in abundance from mid-July to late August and, in fall, the subalpine forests turn gold with Lyall's larches. The tarn-studded tundra, which is flanked by the cliffs of the Monarch Ramparts, offers unparalleled views. It is classic Canadian Rockies scenery, some of the finest anywhere.

Healy Pass and Simpson Pass are easier to access than the Sunshine Meadows,

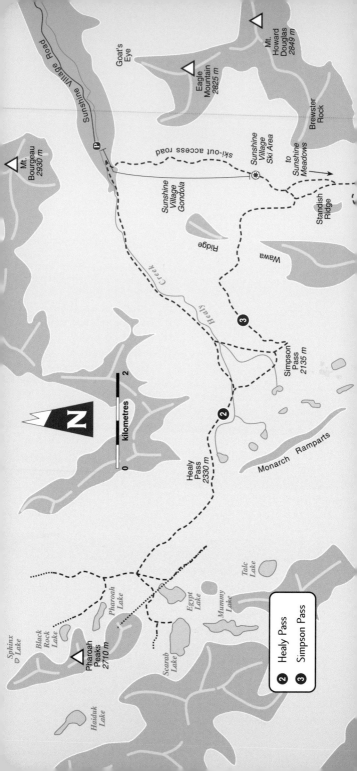

From the northeast end of Healy Pass with Mt. Bourgeau in the distance.

where hikers have to climb an additional 6.5 km (4 mi) up the Sunshine Village access road before hitting the trail. The easy access and proximity to Banff make Healy Pass an ideal dayhike, and, therefore, it is extremely popular.

The Healy Pass and Simpson Pass trailhead is behind the lower gondola terminal. Take the broad cat-track along Healy Creek. After a short distance, turn right onto a more pleasant path, which heads through a dense forest of Englemann spruce and subalpine fir carpeted with feather mosses. The path has an easy to moderate, but steady, grade, up the Healy Creek valley. At 3.1 km (1.9 mi) it crosses Healy Creek, which is a nice rest spot. The damp forest thins somewhat, and the trail winds past several broad avalanche gullies to the north—one of these gullies was the site of a 1990 disaster that killed four skiers. At the next opening, the foundation of an old cabin

(reported to be used by guide/outfitter Bill Peyto) is off to the right, and a backcountry campground with a wooden outhouse and picnic tables comes into view at 5.5 km (3.4 mi).

The first of two junctions for Simpson Pass is 200 m (656 ft) west of the campground. The shorter, lower route—from the junction to Simpson Pass it's 1.3 km (0.8 mi)—heads left at 5.9 km (3.7 mi) from the trailhead. The higher route—from the junction to Simpson Pass it's 2 km (1.2 mi)—splits off at 7.7 km (4.8 mi). Simpson Pass offers a circuit route that connects Healy Pass, Simpson Pass and Sunshine Village. (See page 44 for details.) I prefer the counter clockwise approach, climbing first to Healy Pass and then traversing the alpine tundra to Simpson Pass and down Healy Creek. Or, for those hikers willing to commit to a nine-hour day, it is possible to climb up to Wawa Ridge,

Sunshine Meadows.

from Simpson Pass and then descend into Sunshine Village. Many people prefer to descend into Simpson Pass from Wawa Ridge because of the panoramic views at this higher elevation. To go this route you have to get up to Sunshine Village first and, without the gondola, it's quite tedious.

To get to Simpson Pass, go left at either junction, or continue straight for Healy Pass. The path climbs steeply through the thinning subalpine forest and soon the towering wall of the Monarch Ramparts comes into view. In fall, the lime-green needles of Lyall's larch turn golden, casting a glow, which deepens to resplendent hues of amber and burnt orange before the needles drop in late October.

The trail emerges from the forest and continues to climb into the alpine meadows at the head of Healy Creek. The creek's water carves a course through the alpine tundra. Distinctive boulders covered

in rock lichens stand out against the continuous dense turf of grasses, sedges, mosses and low-lying shrubs of alpine willow and alpine bearberry. Interspersed among them are round, green cushions of pink moss campion and dense mats of yellow and white mountain heather, as well as hardy alpine flowers like fleabanes, western anemones, buttercups, alpine rock cress, purple saxifrage and mountain avens. It is a glorious destination throughout the year.

The second junction with Simpson Pass appears at 7.7 km (4.8 mi). At 9.2 km (5.7 mi), Healy Pass is 'crested' after a final climb through the last stands of scattered pine and larch.

Healy Pass at 2330 m (7642 ft) offers exceptional panoramic views. To the northeast is the Massive Range with Mt. Bourgeau (right) and Mt. Brett (left). The view to the south extends beyond Simpson Pass to the Sunshine Meadows. The towcring peak of Mt. Assiniboine—at 3618 m (11,867 ft), the highest mountain in Banff National Park—looms to the southeast. There are numerous tundra lakes dotting the meadows beneath the long quartzite ridge of the Monarch Ramparts, which stretches between The Monarch at 2904 m (9525 ft) and Healy Pass. To the west are Haiduk Peak and the exquisite Pharaoh Peaks with lakes Egypt, Scarab and Talc nestled below.

From Healy Pass, the trail descends to Egypt Lake campground and a cabin that sleeps 16. The hillside to the north is an easy ascent with even better views of the Egyptian lakes. Pick up the path that leads up the ridge, and climb to the cairn at the top, which is 2545 m (8347 ft) high. Or, if you feel like more off-trail adventure, hike the ridge walk along the crest of the Monarch Ramparts to the south.

As I lay in the alpine meadow the day I hiked this route, a bald eagle appeared in the sky towards Assiniboine. It flew directly to me, swiftly covering territory in a matter of moments that would have taken me several hours to cross. It circled overhead, gliding artfully on the thermals, and, perhaps disappointed that I wasn't prey, it let out a high-pierced cry and vanished into remote Horse Creek Valley beyond. Inspired by the beauty of this pristine wilderness, I decided to extend my hike and headed off to where the eagle appeared: towards Simpson Pass, up Wawa Ridge and into Sunshine Village. From there, I lucked out and got a ride down the access road back to the parking lot.

G.M. Dawson, of the Geological Survey of Canada, named Healy Pass after Captain John Jerome Healy in 1884. Healy travelled extensively throughout Mexico and the West working as a hunter, trapper, guide, soldier, whiskey trader, Indian scout, editor and mining prospector. He was enlisted in the Union Army, had proprietorship of the notorious Fort Whoop-Up in Lethbridge, and was a Montana sheriff. He prospected for gold in Healy Creek, but soon left to seek his fortune elsewhere. He became a manager of operations in Dawson City for the North American Telephone and Telegraph Company, and lived to be an old and wealthy man.

First glimpse of the Monarch Ramparts with dwindling montane forest in the foreground.

3-Simpson Pass

Refer to map on pg. 38.
Difficulty: Moderate
Distance: 5.6 km (3.5 mi) (from Sunshine Village to Simpson Pass)
Ascent Time: 2—3 hours
Elevation Gain: 165 m (541 ft)
Elevation: 2360 m (7741 ft)
Topo Map: Banff 82 0/4
Access: Follow the TransCanada Highway west of Banff for 8.3 km (5 mi) to the Sunshine Village ski resort exit. Follow this road 9 km (5.6 mi) to its end at the gondola parking lot. Begin your hike up the gated access road to the left of the lower gondola terminal. (Although the gondola has transported thousands of hikers to the meadows, it hasn't operated for the past few summers. Call (403) 762—4000 or 762—6500 for current information.)

Easy access and classic Canadian Rockies scenery make Simpson Pass a very popular dayhike. There are essentially two approaches to Simpson Pass. Hikers can either take the historic route used by George Simpson that heads up the Healy Creek trail from the Sunshine Village parking lot—this route intersects the Simpson Pass trail at 5.9 km (3.7 mi) and 7.7 km (4.8 mi) (see page 39)—or take the 9-km (5.6 mi) access road up to Sunshine Village ski resort and descend into Simpson Pass from Wawa Ridge. Many consider the latter route to be the most scenic, but with panoramic views of this magnitude, any direction looks good!

To get to Wawa Ridge, begin your hike up the gated

Yellow paintbrushes with scorpionweed.

and the towering precipice of Mt. Assiniboine to the southeast. The Monarch and the Monarch Ramparts are to the southwest, and the Massive Range is to the northeast.

From the ridge, the trail descends off the back into the subalpine forest and contours around the rocky escarpment high above Healy Creek, before dropping into the open meadows at Simpson Pass (2135 m/7003 ft) at 5.6 km (3.8 mi). A word of caution— this trail can be very wet in the early season or during rainy weather. Simpson Pass is an open, grassy meadow that in mid-summer looks like a painting by an Impressionist: a blend of pink, purple, fuschia, blue, lavender, yellow and white. Daisies, violets, larkspur, lousewort, bluebells, Indian paintbrush, fireweed, valerian, woolly everlastings, wild vetch, columbines, harebells and forget-me-nots grow with wild determination.

Here the trail forks. The lower route to the right cuts across to the Healy Pass trail, and provides a quick exit route to the Sunshine Village parking lot. (Those hikers doing the Healy/Simpson Pass circuit from the Healy Creek side usually descend at this point on their way back from Healy Pass.) It is well worth continuing straight ahead, into the B.C. side of Simpson

access road to the left of the lower gondola terminal. The 6.5-km (4-mi), steep, gravel road to Sunshine Village ski resort is somewhat monotonous with limited views. Goat's Eye station is at 4.2 km (2.6 mi), and the upper gondola terminal is at 6.5 km (4 mi).

From the upper gondola terminal, walk downhill to the Wawa Ridge T-bar ski lift (to the right of the Sunshine Village Interpretive Centre), and follow the 1.9-km (1.2-mi) Meadow Park trail heading uphill to the north.

The trail climbs quickly above treeline and onto the rocky crest of Wawa Ridge at 1.9 km (1.2 mi). From this vantage point, the view is superb and encompasses Sunshine Meadows, Citadel Pass

Sir George Simpson (b. Scotland 1787; d. Lachine, Québec, 1860) was born an illegitimate son of Scottish descent. He had a distinguished career with the Hudson's Bay Company. In 1820, he left London for what was then called Rupert's Land. Here, he travelled extensively along the early fur trade routes across what is now Canada, and developed a knowledge of the fur trade never before equalled. In 1841, he was knighted and appointed governor of the Hudson's Bay Company.

Simpson visited the Canadian Rockies enroute around the world—by horse, boat and foot—an account published in his book *Narrative of a Journey Around the World During the Years 1841 and 1842* (2 vols. London, 1847). He passed through what was originally called Shuswap Pass, travelling from the Bow River down into the Kootenay Valley. James Hector later renamed it Simpson Pass. In 1904, a group of people camped at the pass found Simpson's initials carved into a fallen tree (which now resides at the museum in Banff). Simpson hoped to use the pass for the company's fur expeditions to Oregon, but an easier route was found further west. After 1833, Simpson made his home at Lachine, outside of Montréal.

Pass, towards Healy Pass. At this point the trail disappears into another dense subalpine forest, carpeted with feather mosses, clubmosses, lichens and shade-loving plants such as delicate twinflowers, fairy bells, bronze bells, bunchberry, kinnikinnik and wintergreens, before ascending through thinning canopy into Healy Meadows. This area is classic alpine tundra with heath tundra, sphagnum moss, jewel-like tarns, bubbling brooks, alpine larches and stands of gnarled and stunted trees, all which lie alongside the enormous quartzite wall of the Monarch Ramparts.

At 6 km (3.7 mi), the trail to Eohippus Lake, with its sapphire-blue waters, branches off to the right. The 3.2-km (2-mi) trail is a good option for strong hikers. At 7.7 km (4.8 mi), the path merges with the Healy Pass trail. Continue for 1.5 km (0.93 mi) to crest Healy Pass with its superlative views, or descend Healy Creek to the Sunshine Village parking lot.

4-Sunshine Meadows/ Citadel Pass

Sunshine Village parking lot to Rock Isle Lake

Difficulty: Moderate; strenuous dayhike
Distance: 8.1 km (5 mi)
Ascent Time: 3.5 hrs
Elevation Gain: 570 m (1870 ft)
Elevation: 2300 m (7544 ft)

Sunshine Village parking lot to Larix Lake

Difficulty: Moderate; strenuous dayhike
Distance: 9.7 km (6 mi)
Ascent Time: 4 hours
Elevation Gain: 570 m (1870 ft)
Elevation: 2300 m (7544 ft)

Sunshine Village parking lot to Citadel Pass

Difficulty: Difficult; strenuous dayhike
Distance: 15.9 km (9.8 mi)
Ascent Time: 5–6 hours
Elevation Gain: 685 m (2247 ft)
Elevation: 2360 m (7740 ft)

Topo Map: Banff 82 O/4 (trail incorrectly marked)
Access: Follow the TransCanada Highway west of Banff for 8.3 km (5.1 mi) to the Sunshine Village ski resort exit. Follow this road for 9 km (5.6 mi) to its end at the gondola parking lot. Begin your hike up the gated access road to the left of the lower gondola terminal. (Although the gondola has transported thousands of hikers to the meadows, it hasn't operated for the past few summers. Call (403) 762-4000 or 762-6500 for current information.)

Rock Isle Lake.

Sunshine Meadows is one of the most scenic locations in the Canadian Rockies. It is known for its sublime landscapes and resplendent wildflowers. The lush terrain consists of subalpine meadows and dense alpine tundra, and is part of an extensive alpine meadow system—the largest in the world—stretching some 15 km (9.3 mi), at an average elevation of 2225 m (7298 ft), along the Continental Divide between Citadel Pass and the Monarch Ramparts at Healy Pass. The Continental Divide is a mountain ridge that divides waters flowing east and north to the Arctic and Atlantic oceans from those flowing west to the Pacific. It is a unique ecoregion, in part because of the intense precipitation blowing over the mountains from the Pacific. The weather creates a moist environment in a place that would usually be rock and glacial ice; consequently, an astonishing variety of alpine flowers grow here, of which some are specific to the area. There are many places to explore in the Sunshine Meadows, but the three main routes lead to either Rock Isle Lake, Citadel Pass or Simpson Pass via Wawa Ridge.

The 6.5-km (4-mi), steep, gravel road to the Sunshine Village ski resort is dull, with not much to look at. If you

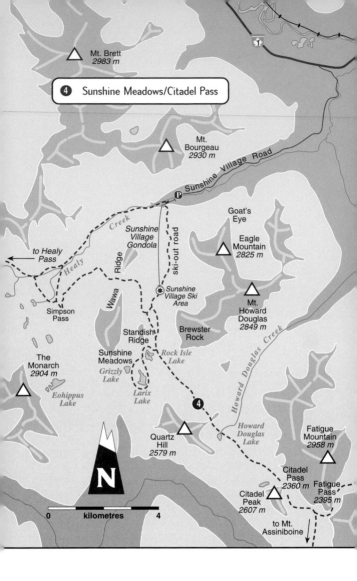

Mt. Brett
2983 m

4 Sunshine Meadows/Citadel Pass

Mt. Bourgeau
2930 m

Sunshine Village Road

P

Creek

Sunshine Village Gondola

ski-out road

Goat's Eye

Eagle Mountain
2825 m

to Healy Pass

Healy

Wawa Ridge

Sunshine Village Ski Area

Mt. Howard Douglas
2849 m

Simpson Pass

Standish Ridge

Brewster Rock

Howard Douglas Creek

The Monarch
2904 m

Sunshine Meadows

Grizzly Lake

Rock Isle Lake

Eohippus Lake

Larix Lake

4

Howard Douglas Lake

Fatigue Mountain
2958 m

Quartz Hill
2579 m

N

0   kilometres   4

Citadel Pass
2360 m

Fatigue Pass
2395 m

Citadel Peak
2607 m

to Mt. Assiniboine

have a mountain bike, you might consider doing the 40-minute ride to the Village, where you can leave your bike for the return trip. Although the bike ride up is still a slog, it is far less tedious than walking, and the ride out is fast and wild. Goat's Eye station is at 4.2 km (2.6 mi), and the upper gondola terminal is at 6.5 km (4 mi). Once at the Village, continue walking (south) straight ahead on the crushed rock path, to the left of the old day lodge and Sunshine Ski School building. Fifteen metres (49 ft) past the

Mt. Assiniboine was named in 1885 by Dr. G.M. Dawson of the Geological Survey of Canada in honour of the Stoney, an Assiniboine tribe living near Banff whose name means 'those who cook by placing hot rocks in water.' In 1845 Father de Smet and his guides were probably the first Euro-Americans to see the peak. There have been many expeditions to climb the peak, but it was Sir James Outram, with Swiss guides, who finally made the first successful ascent in 1901.

Parks Canada Avalanche Control station, the path branches left and climbs steadily uphill through an open larch forest to the summit of the Great Divide, which is 1.1 km (0.68 mi) from the ski resort. Standish Ridge is on your right, and Brewster Rock is on your left.

The junction to Rock Isle and Grizzly and Larix lakes is at 7.6 km (4.7 mi). Hikers not going on to Citadel Pass should turn right and proceed to the Rock Isle Lake viewpoint at 8.1 km (5 mi). Or, for more adventure, do the Grizzly and Larix lakes circuit, an extra 4.2 km (2.6 mi), by turning left at the trail sign at 8.3 km (5.1 mi). For a higher elevation, continue straight ahead for 0.5 km (0.31 mi) at the Grizzly/Larix junction, turn right at the Standish junction, and hike another 50 m (164 ft) to the viewing platform at the top of Standish Ridge.

From here, you can either retrace your steps to the junction, or continue along Meadow Park trail for 1.6 km (0.99 mi) to another junction that takes you back to Sunshine Village (6.5 km/4 mi). Once up here, however, it is well worth hiking the 300 m (984 ft) to the top of Wawa Ridge for unprecedented views of the entire region. Strong hikers may want to descend into Simpson Pass and take the Healy Creek trail back to the gondola terminal in the Sunshine Village parking lot, making for a more interesting circuit route. (See page 36 for the Healy Pass hike.)

Hikers doing the strenuous full-day hike to Citadel Pass should stay left at the 7.6-km (4.7-mi) junction. Parks Canada went to great expense to fly gravel in by helicopter to build these trails, so stay on them to protect the delicate ecosystem and surrounding vegetation from cro-

Mt. Assiniboine.

sion. The gravel path traverses gentle, rolling meadows for 3.9 km (2.4 mi) before reaching Quartz Ridge.

In mid-summer, there must be more flowers up here than anywhere else on earth. The alpine tundra resembles a green sponge constructed of grasses, sedges and mosses, low-lying woody shrubs of alpine willow and kinnikinnik and dense mats of the miniature evergreen mountain heather. Exotic alpine wildflowers such as moss campion, valerian, fleabane, everlastings, western anemone, buttercups, glacier lilies and orchids saturate the heath with intense colour. Even the glacial erratics are covered in the vivid pigment of rock lichens. By late September, the chromatic hues fade to sepia tones, turning the meadows brown as far as the eye can see.

While the world may seem perfectly benign up here on the Continental Divide, be aware that major weather systems can blow in at any moment. Clear blue skies can become sullen and overcast. Even on a brilliant summer day, fierce winds bringing rain, sleet, hail and whiteout

On a clear day, the majestic snow-capped peak of Mt. Assiniboine—3618 m (11,867 ft) high—with the customary plume soaring from its zenith, is visible from most high elevations in Banff National Park. Towering above the neighbouring peaks, Assiniboine has become an icon for adventure in the backcountry. Its sublime beauty embodies the spirit of wilderness.

Situated on the Continental Divide, 35 km (22 mi) south of Banff, Mt. Assiniboine is often referred to as the 'Matterhorn of the Rockies.' The horn-shaped mountain is the sixth highest peak in the Canadian Rockies and the highest in both Banff National Park and Assiniboine Provincial Park.

blizzards are not uncommon in an afternoon. Be prepared; worse than being wet and chilly, you could become hypothermic, with no short escape route out.

After a long traverse across the meadows, the trail descends into a hollow before climbing a set of switchbacks through a subalpine forest of larch, spruce and Douglas fir. At 11.5 km (7 mi), the trail continues up to the ridge below Quartz Hill, which is 2579 m (8461 ft) high. Bright green wolf lichen hangs from the dead Lyall's larch trees, making a striking contrast with the golden needles in fall. The gravel path ends, and an eroded trail descends south to Howard Douglas Lake (called 'Sundown Lake' on the topographical map) and a backcountry campground on the east shore of the lake (12.3 km/7.6 mi). The trail continues up a narrow defile, through more meadows filled with subalpine and alpine flowers, and past many small lakes before reaching Citadel Pass (15.9 km/9.9 mi).

The late September day I visited Citadel Pass was blustery with purple thunderheads looming to the northwest. It meant I couldn't stay long, even though Fatigue Pass (2395 m/7855 ft), uphill to the left, can be reached in less than one hour. I turned my back on the Lake Og trail to Mt. Assiniboine, which is 17 km (11 mi) in the distance, with its steep descent into the Valley of the Rocks, and headed back to Sunshine Village through biting winds and pelting rain. I was thankful for the extra warm clothes in my pack.

From Cory Pass looking towards the trail. Mt. Edith is to the left.

5- Cory Pass/Edith Pass

Difficulty: Difficult; very steep
sections
Distance: 7.9 km (4.9 mi);
13.4-km (8.3-mi) circuit route
Ascent Time: 3.5–4 hrs (5-hr
circuit route)
Elevation Gain: 950 m (3116 ft)
Elevation: 2360 m (7740 ft)
Topo Map: Banff 82 O/4

Access: Take the Bow Valley
Parkway exit (Highway 1A),
5.7 km (3.5 mi) west of the
Banff/Mt. Norquay interchange
on the TransCanada Highway.
Turn right in 3 km (1.9 mi), and
follow the access road to its
end at the Fireside picnic area.
The Cory/Edith Pass trailhead
is located at the bridge, which
crosses the creek into the
picnic site.

Set in the serrated lime-stone peaks of the Sawback Range, Mt. Louis, with its dogtooth spire, is one of the most spectacular, and unusual, peaks in the area. Despite the arduous trek on this hike, it is well worth the effort to get a glimpse of this striking obelisk. Hikers can approach Mt. Louis from two directions: via the gentler Edith Pass or the super-steep Cory Pass. A circuit route is possible; either direction takes you through diverse ecological terrain, shifting from the lower montane valley, through dense subalpine forests, to alpine meadows above the treeline, and finally through a land of scree and sentinels in the Gargoyle Valley.

Many hikers consider Cory Pass to be extremely arduous, regardless of whether you climb up through the Gargoyle Valley or via the

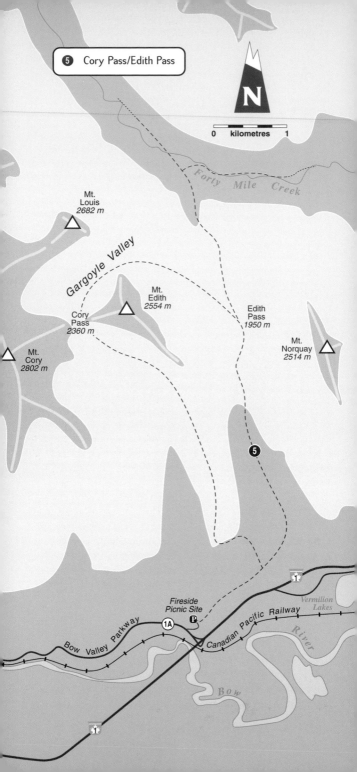

5 Cory Pass/Edith Pass

N

0   kilometres   1

Forty Mile Creek

Mt.
Louis
2682 m

Gargoyle Valley

Mt.
Edith
2554 m

Cory
Pass
2360 m

Edith
Pass
1950 m

Mt.
Norquay
2514 m

Mt. Cory
2802 m

5

*Fireside
Picnic Site*

P

*Vermilion
Lakes*

1A

Bow Valley Parkway

Canadian Pacific Railway

River

1

Bow

1

Gargoyle pinnacles of Eldon limestone at Cory Pass.

southwest slope. People with weak knees might consider going as far as Edith Pass and then retracing their steps. I have done the hike from both directions and prefer the clockwise circuit, which heads up the southwest slope, to get the uphill climbing over with at the outset and have a less extreme descent at the end of the day. Either way, the Cory Pass section is mercilessly steep.

Those hikers who can endure the steep switchbacks and one short cliff band section will be rewarded with interesting rock formations and superlative views that high elevation brings. I did this hike on a beautiful mid-September day, and was thankful for the cool fall breeze that kept my body temperature down. Only the extremely hardy would want to do the exposed climb to Cory Pass under a blistering sun. There is no water on the front side.

From the trailhead, cross the bridge over a creek and pass through the lovely Fireside picnic area with a large stone fireplace. Continue for 200 m (220 yd) on an old road through the montane forest of aspen, Douglas fir and white spruce. Turn left (north) and continue to the Cory Pass

Mt. Louis is named in honour of Louis Beaufort Stewart (1861–1937), a professor of Surveying and Geodesy at the University of Toronto. He accompanied Coleman, president of both the Royal Society of Canada and the Geological Society of America, on his forays into the West in 1892 and 1903.

Looking up towards Cory Pass from mid-way on the trail. A good rest spot.

junction at 1.1 km (0.68 mi) where the circuit begins.

Cory Pass is uphill, to the left. Edith Pass is straight ahead. The most direct route to Cory Pass heads north up a steep, grassy slope filled with wildflowers and dotted with lodgepole pine and 'noisy leaf' trembling aspen. Western wood lily, Indian paintbrush, gaillardia, wild blue flax, nodding onion, Hooker's thistle, field chickweed, sweet vetch, Solomon's seal, fireweed, yarrow and sage cover the dry south slope.

A word of caution—the Rocky Mountain wood tick thrives in the montane ecoregion from early April to mid-June. These flat, spider-like creatures climb grasses and shrubs awaiting their prey. This means you! A bite from this nasty insect can be dangerous and cause Rocky Mountain spotted fever, which is sometimes fatal, or tick paralysis, which can cause nervous system disorders. Wear a hat and make sure to have a friend check you carefully for ticks. If you find one, dislodge it carefully to avoid separating its body from the head and leaving the mouth attached to you.

The trail is extremely steep—straight up with no switchbacks. Fortunately, most of it is in the shade. After what seems like an eternity, you emerge out of the dense canopy of spruce and fir onto the south ridge of Mt. Edith (2.4 km/1.5 mi). This area is a good rest spot from which to survey the Bow Corridor. There are great views of Vermilion Lakes, the Muleshoe, the Sundance Range and Mt. Assiniboine to the south. Scattered in the

Cory Pass scree slopes.

open woods are many wildflowers and berry bushes, including red osier dogwood, Indian paintbrush, fireweed and buffaloberry. The quality of sage, creeping juniper and common juniper, with their silvery-purple berries, is exceptional.

From here, you climb gradually before descending a notch, or cliff band, which some hikers find intimidating. Then begin the traverse across the open avalanche slopes of Mt. Edith towards Cory Pass (6 km/3.7 mi).

At Cory Pass there are two talus slopes, which make a perfect V-shape. The col (2360 m/7741 ft) is very dramatic with craggy peaks often silhouetted in the late afternoon sun. Only tenacious alpine flowers, which can survive on the wind-scoured scree slopes, exist here: purple saxifrage, golden fleabane, Lyall's rock cress, yellow and white mountain avens, western anemone, moss campion and stonecrop.

Mt. Cory is named after yet another politician, William Wallace Cory (1865–1943), Deputy Minister of the Interior from 1905–30. The summit was once known as Hole-in-the-Wall, because of the large cave below the south ridge visible from the west.

The adjacent alpine meadow with its stands of krummholz spruce, lichen-covered rocks and abundance of alpine flowers make this place an idyllic lunch spot on sunny days. The narrow, rocky pass with the gargoyles—pinnacles of Eldon limestone—provides protection from the wind. The view is breathtaking in all directions. It overlooks the Bow Valley, with Mt. Bourgeau and Assiniboine to the south, Sulphur and Rundle to the east and Castle and Temple to the west.

There is plenty of terrain for those hikers who enjoy scrambling. Mt. Edith has three different summits of varying difficulty. The North and Centre Peaks offer moderate scrambling from Cory Pass, and the South Peak is more demanding with some exposure and 1120 m (3674 ft) gain in height. Mt. Cory is an easy scramble via the south ridge, but the trailhead is back down on Highway 1A, 1.9 km (1.2 mi) from the southeast junction with the Trans-Canada Highway.

Hikers continuing on to Edith Pass should descend the steep col into Gargoyle Valley on the scree path that hugs the north slope of Mt. Edith. The long traverse winds through the monochromatic valley, flanked by gigantic, grey, vertical slabs of Palliser limestone, past the striking obelisk of Mt. Louis (2682 m/8797 ft), the scenic focal point of the hike, on the left. Mt. Louis stands like a resistant tower, while surrounding rock has eroded away. Mountain sheep leave traces of their agility etched across the steep talus slopes of this dogtooth spire. I feel assured that the ghostly fingers of development will never cast their shadow here.

The steep scree switchbacks contour around the slabby north rib of Mt. Edith (2554 m/8377 ft) and into the mouth of the Gargoyle Valley. (Stay high to avoid the drainage to Forty Mile Creek, especially if late-lying snow obscures the path.) The trail crosses an avalanche slope—which provides a few

Mt. Edith

moments of glissading fun— before descending through tall patches of cow parsnip, yarrow, fireweed, Solomon's seal, and numerous berry shrubs, to the forested summit of Edith Pass below. This high route reaches the summit of Edith Pass some 500 m (1640 ft) north of the junction. There are great views of Mt. Norquay and into the Forty Mile Creek valley.

The trail levels out in a subalpine forest of spruce and Douglas fir and soon intersects the Edith Pass junction. (The Edith Pass hike offers three options: a 6-km (3.7-mi) hike to view Mt. Louis; a 13-km (8-mi) circuit route through Edith Pass, the Gargoyle Valley and Cory Pass; or the forested lower route through Edith Pass to Forty Mile Creek—the headwaters are 15 km (9 mi) to the north—looping back to the Mt. Norquay ski area, 6.9 km (4.8 mi) from the parking lot.

So, the trail either climbs back up Cory Pass, continues north to Forty Mile Creek, or descends to the parking lot 4 km (2.9 mi) below. Having just descended the narrow Gargoyle Valley, your shaky quads, no doubt, will beg you to continue downhill into the cool, damp forest of trembling aspen, lodgepole pine and white spruce. At the edge of the ravine I saw a deer caught in the light streaming through the trees, before it moved deeper into the forest. Several species of orchids grow along the gentle pine needle path that winds through the emerald and peridot-coloured forest floor. Moss banks muffle the sparkling waters of Edith Creek, leading back to the old road and the picnic site. It is a magical place, and a perfect way to end a brilliant day.

Aspen at the beginning of the Muleshoe trail.

6-Muleshoe

Difficulty: Easy to moderate;
with steep sections
Distance: 1.1 km (0.68 mi)
Ascent Time: 30 minutes
Elevation Gain: 65 m (213 m)
Elevation: 90 m (295 ft)
Topo Map: Banff 82 0/4

Access: The Muleshoe parking
area is also a pleasant picnic site
located on the S.W. side of the
Bow Valley Parkway (Highway
1A). It's 5.5 km (3.4 mi) from
the junction with the
TransCanada Highway, which is
10.7 km (6.6 ft) west of the
Banff/Mt. Norquay junction, or
18.7 km (12 mi) east of Castle
Junction. The trail is located
across the road from the
parking lot/picnic area.

The Muleshoe refers to the arm shaped like a horseshoe in the Bow River. This formation was created when a river eroded deeply into the valley bottom and abandoned the bend for a more direct route, leaving behind pools called ox-bow lakes. The stagnating ponds are home to beaver, muskrat, moose and numerous birds, including osprey.

The short Muleshoe Trail begins in dense stands of trembling aspen, a tree common in the montane zone of the front ranges. The trail winds through a prescribed burn site, where lodgepole pine and aspen grow among the charred remains of ancient Douglas fir, before climbing the scenic southwest slope of Mt. Cory to the expansive meadows 200 m (656 ft) above the trailhead.

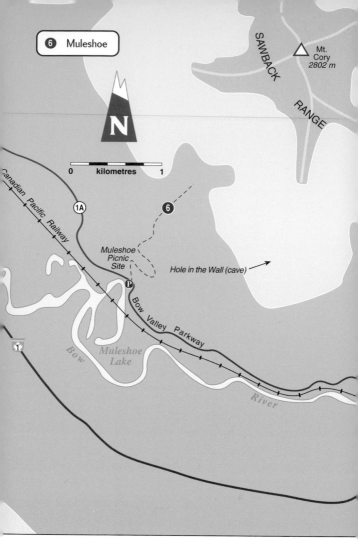

Prescribed burns are done by Parks Canada as a means of rejuvenating a forest. Cones require a certain heat level before opening and spreading their seeds. If there has been a shortage of natural fires, forest management starts one. Aside from being an interesting science project in wilderness management, the charred tree trunks with exfoliating bark, which emerge from a sea of wildflowers, have a stark and beautiful look. They stand solemnly, like mute guardians, attending to the playful, swaying heads of western wood lily, Indian paintbrush, yellow and blue clematis, gaillardia,

Prescribed burn site.

wild blue flax, Solomon's seal, fireweed and yarrow.

At 1.1 km (0.7 mi), the easy-to-moderate trail ends at the base of a hillside overlooking Bow River and Muleshoe Lake. A hiking sign indicates the way back. From here, a steep animal track continues up the exposed slope to a grassy meadow. Two of this trail's best features are numerous wildflowers in summer and unobstructed, sweeping views of the Bow Valley from Castle Mountain near Lake Louise, to Mt. Rundle beside the Banff townsite.

For hikers with stamina, a less obvious animal path continues up a minor ridge with many scenic views, and into a subalpine forest before emerging on the west ridge of Mt. Cory, which is 2200 m (7216 ft) high. And indeed, sections of this trail are as steep as the path to Cory Pass. Take water, because there is none up here.

The Muleshoe makes an ideal early season hike; the snow vanishes from the sun-warmed southern slopes by May. Hikers should check themselves for the Rocky Mountain wood tick. The potentially dangerous insect can cause Rocky Mountain spotted fever or nervous disorders, if it attaches to your skin, the complications of which can be fatal. Wear a hat and have a friend check your body thoroughly at the end of the hike.

Trembling Aspen (White Poplar)

Dense stands of trembling aspen are a common site in the Canadian Rockies, especially in the montane ecoregion of the front ranges. Natives call the aspen 'noisy leaf.' Standing amongst the trembling leaves, it's a descriptive name.

The Blackfeet tell the following legend about how aspens came to tremble. All the plants and animals respected their creator, Napi. Whenever he appeared the trees would bow, partly out of respect and partly out of fear. One day the aspens got together and decided that Napi wasn't so important and agreed that they would not bow when he walked amongst them. Sure enough, the next day they stood boldly in his presence. Napi was furious, and threw lighting bolts at them, almost scaring the leaves off their branches. To this day, the aspens are so scared that every time they hear someone walking in the woods they tremble their leaves in fear.

Hikers no doubt marvel about the abundance of plants growing in the Canadian Rockies, and might wonder if there is a medicinal use for them. Native tribes in the area had a use for almost every plant, and each part of the plant as well. The aspen is no different.

The Cree used the buds, inner bark and leaves as medicine. Aspen tea was a good tonic, and was used in treatment of rheumatism, diarrhea, liver and kidney problems. The Woods Cree boiled the shredded inner bark to make a medicinal tea for treating coughs and the outer bark for treatment of venereal disease. The white powder from the bark stopped bleeding. A spoonful of aspen bark and tree fungus stopped earaches. Chewed leaves were plastered on insect stings to draw out the venom. Young seeds were used by women trying to induce miscarriages. The pulpy material under the bark was a special treat for children. Aspen wood was used to make canoe paddles, bowls and teepee frames. The Chipewan burned green aspen wood and extracted lye, which they combined with caribou fat to make soap. Herbalists from many cultures use the leaves and inner bark for stomach pain, liver problems and headaches, but its greatest effects are on the urinary/genital system. The inner bark is used to strengthen weakened female organs (especially during excessive menstrual bleeding). A tincture of the bark has been used for fevers, rheumatism, arthritis, colds, urinary infections and diarrhea.

Aspen is also the preferred food of beavers and ungulates, many of which eat the protective outer bark and leave behind black scars. Small aspens are also used by elk and deer before fall rut; they remove the velvet linings on their antlers by running against the trees.

As seen from the East End of Rundle, the backside of Chinaman's Peak.

7-Chinaman's Peak

Difficulty: Difficult hike; easy scramble
Distance: 1.6 km (0.99 mi)
Ascent Time: 1—2 hrs
Elevation Gain: 700 m (2296 ft)
Elevation: 2408 m (7898 ft)
Topo Map: 82 0/3 Canmore

Access: Follow the Smith-Dorrien/Spray Trail (Highway 742) from the Canmore townsite, past the Canmore Nordic Centre to the Goat Creek Trail parking lot at Whiteman's Gap.

Hikers who like to reach peaks without technical climbing will enjoy Chinaman's Peak. It gets you high, real fast. It is a short, steep hike to incredible views: Canmore townsite and Bow Valley; the east end of Mt. Rundle, Goat Creek valley and the Spray Lakes; and Assiniboine, Bourgeau and Temple tower in the distance.

While the ascent is steep, it is still more of a hike for the two-legged than a scramble. But some light bouldering can be done on dolomite slabs near the top. This climb is not for hikers wanting a leisurely day; the extreme ascent and often crowded summit make it more of a rugged workout than a restful trip.

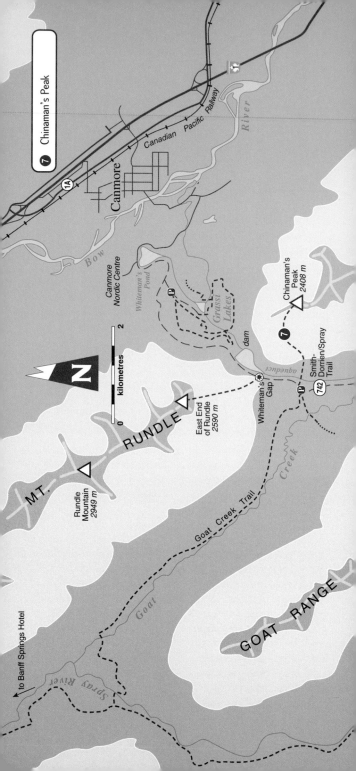

7 Chinaman's Peak

Canmore

Canadian Pacific Railway

Bow

River

1A

Canmore Nordic Centre

Whiteman's Pond

Grassi Lakes

P

Chinaman's Peak
2408 m

7

dam

aqueduct

Whiteman's Gap

Smith-
Dorrien/Spray
Trail

P

742

N

0   kilometres   2

East End
of Rundle
2590 m

MT.   RUNDLE

Rundle Mountain
2949 m

Goat Creek Trail

Goat   Creek

GOAT   RANGE

Goat

Spray River

to Banff Springs Hotel

Montane forest of Douglas fir, lodgepole pine and spruce.

The trailhead is located across the highway from the Goat Creek parking lot. Cross the bridge over the canal and walk to the end of a gravel road to a service hut. The trail begins beside the hut and plunges instantly into a dark montane forest of Douglas fir, lodgepole pine and spruce. A lovely pine needle path carves through a thick, moist carpet of feather mosses, clubmosses and lichens—pale green *Usnea* and black *Bryoria*—which hang like hair from dead lodgepole pines. The dainty Calypso orchid or the mini-ature, lacy mitrewort is hidden in the emerald-green mounds. Other shade-loving plants such as delicate twinflowers, fairy bells, bronze bells, bunchberry, kinnikinnik and wintergreens grow along the path and beneath the dense spruce and fir canopy.

The well-worn and often eroded path immediately heads upward. It climbs the southwest slope of this over-thrust mountain by going up the left side of a slabby creek bed. The ascent is so extreme that the trail doesn't even switchback until long after your calf muscles are aching. There are numerous shortcuts on badly eroded trails. Keep to the right. The path continues through the thinning coniferous forest and emerges above the treeline 45 minutes later, 500 m (1640 ft) from the start. It is a good place for a snack.

From here, you can either take the easier, more gradual route to the right and traverse the scree to the col, which then winds along the southeast ridge to the summit, or continue 300 m (984 ft) directly ahead. This last route goes up the scree over large boulders and limestone slabs to reach the summit approximately one hour later. Either way is intense.

The cairn sits atop a spectacular horseshoe cirque, which overlooks the sheer northeast face of Chinaman's Peak. Be careful close to the edge; the precipice can induce vertigo. For a thrill, I like to lie on my stomach and peer down the vertical walls to the Bow Valley below. It is easy to envision the flight of an eagle gliding on thermals.

Or bring a parachute—Chinaman's Peak has become a popular launch site for paragliders. You are likely to see other extreme sport enthusiasts here, such as rock climbers who have just scaled the face to emerge covered in chalk over the ledge. A short ridge walk to the left leads you to a very cool rock bivouac, presumably built as an emergency shelter to protect climbers in inclement weather. It's also possible to traverse the ridge to a southern peak, although it is much more difficult than the route up and requires some route-finding. Once there, it is an easy ascent down to the canal via the west slopes.

Bald Eagle

Route up Chinaman's Peak where treeline ends and boulders and scree begin.

There is as much controversy over who first climbed Chinaman's Peak, and in what year, as there is over the name, which some find to be a racial slur. Local legend and sketchy newspaper articles seem to agree that it was a person of Chinese descent, but it is disputed who it was—either a man called Ha Ling or Lee Poon. Both men were Chinese cooks working in the Oskaloosa Hotel, a single miners' residence in Canmore.

Rumour has it that Ha Ling was challenged to do the climb in 10 hours and bets were laid that he couldn't. Apparently, he did the round trip in six hours, by following the old pack trail up through Grassi Lakes to Whiteman's Gap and then up the southwest slope to the summit. For his efforts he received $50, no small sum in 1888, and the promise that the peak be named Ha Ling Peak in his honour—a broken promise.

The name Chinaman's Peak has become a thorn in the hide of the politically correct, and has provoked a prominent Calgary lawyer, Alfred Chow, to request a name change from the Historical Resources Board. Some Canmore residents maintain that it honours the numerous men of Chinese descent who worked for the Canmore Mines.

The East End of Rundle (showing scree and talus slopes), as seen from Chinaman's Peak.

8-East End of Rundle

Difficulty: Difficult hike;
easy scramble
Distance: 2.6 km (1.6 mi)
Ascent Time: 2–4 hrs
Height Gain: 950 m (3116 ft)
Elevation: 2590 m (8495 ft)
Topo Map: 82 0/3 Canmore

Access: Follow the Smith-
Dorrien/Spray Trail (Highway
742) from the Canmore
townsite, past the Canmore
Nordic Centre, to the Goat
Creek Trail parking lot at
Whiteman's Gap.

eaching the eastern peak of Mt. Rundle involves an intense climb on a good trail up the south ridge to the shoulder, an easy scramble up cliff bands to an alpine meadow, and climbing a steep scree path up the talus slopes to the summit. It is more difficult than Chinaman's Peak, and is not a leisurely hike. It is defi-nitely arduous. This hike is a good season-opener, because the snow usually disappears by mid-May.

From the Goat Creek parking lot, hike back along the road towards Canmore. Look for an unmarked trail on the west side of the highway near the first set of power line poles. The hike begins with an intense climb through

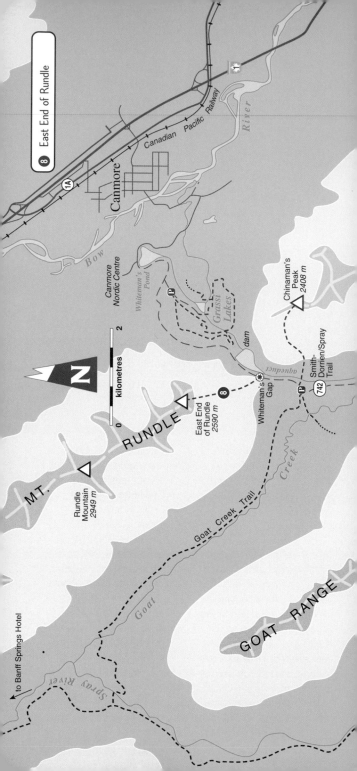

N

kilometres

0   2

Bow   River

1A

Canmore

Canadian Pacific Railway

Canmore Nordic Centre

Whiteman's Pond

Grassi Lakes

dam

aqueduct

Chinaman's Peak 2408 m

Smith-Dorrien/Spray Trail

742

Whiteman's Gap

East End of Rundle 2590 m

8

MT.

RUNDLE

Rundle Mountain 2949 m

Goat Creek Trail

Goat   Creek

GOAT RANGE

Goat

Spray River

to Banff Springs Hotel

Cliff bands.

a montane forest on a newly constructed trail up to the south ridge. At the ridge it turns right and continues through the ever-thinning forest to the treeline. It goes up short, vertical limestone slabs, with route options for all levels of climbers, and across a ramp that leads to the shoulder. The route is fun and moves through varied terrain, although it is exposed most of the way and could be unpleasant in extreme heat or inclement weather. There is little protection and no water.

Just beyond the shoulder is an alpine meadow with an abundance of wildflowers in mid-summer: pale blue alpine forget-me-not, blue larkspur, yellow buttercup, pink fireweed, white camas, purple scorpion weed, Siberian aster and mountain sorrel, to name a few. This meadow makes a lyrical lunch spot nestled amongst lichen-laced boulders and islands of stunted spruce, known as krummholz ('crooked wood' in German). Alpine bearberry, juniper, crowberry, alpine willow, moss campion and mountain heather grow on rocky outcrops seeking protection from the wind. The talus slopes

Alpine flowers on a scree slope.

higher up are home to the delicate alpine blossoms of purple saxifrage, golden fleabane, Lyall's rock cress, yellow and white mountain avens and stonecrop, which tenaciously cling to the scree.

Finally, scree paths branch out in different directions to the summit, 2.6 km (1.6 mi) from the trailhead. I took the one to the right and climbed the steep talus slopes and cliff bands to crest the summit. This peak is not Rundle's true summit, but the most eastern peak.

The view is outstanding and not only encompasses Chinaman's Peak with Kananaskis country beyond, but the Goat, Sundance, Sawback and Massive mountain ranges with the horn peak of Assiniboine towering on the horizon. The view also includes the Fairholme Range, with Mt. Inglismaldie, Lady Macdonald, Cougar and Car-

rot creeks and part of the more obscure Ghost region beyond.

There are two minor summits at the east end of Rundle with many opportunities for some excellent scrambling and ridge walks. The vertiginous ridge drops abruptly down the sheer north face into bowl-shaped cirques and U-shaped valleys below. For the most part, it is very do-able and safe, but take care in the loose scree above the cliff bands. This area is the eastern end of the Rundle traverse, a 12-km (7.4-mi) ridge walk that requires ropes and some technical climbing in certain sections.

We went as far as the second peak and tried for a third, but got intimidated on some cliff bands and decided to turn back. We retraced our steps to the second minor summit, then traversed the southwest slopes of shattered, brown

Drainage gully between the East End of Rundle and Chinaman's Peak.

shale to connect with the scree path, which drops down the cliffs and into the meadows below. There are many places on Rundle to go terribly wrong. It's best to stay high and stick to the sometimes vague, but established trail; otherwise it's easy to slide on the loose scree and plummet off cliff bands into drainage gullies below.

Mt. Rundle is an over-thrust mountain that is typical in the front ranges. It features a tilted southwest slope and a steep northeast cliff, and looks like an old writing desk. This type of mountain illustrates how the thrust sheet slid up-wards and over one another during the Laramide Orogeny in the Cenozoic era 65 million years ago.

James Hector, the geologist on the Palliser Expedition, named Mt. Rundle in honour of Robert Terrill Rundle (1811–96), the first Methodist missionary to arrive in the Bow Valley. From 1840, Rundle travelled among both the native tribes of the Rockies and the Plains. In 1844 he arrived in the Canadian Rockies. Although Rundle greatly respected the Cree—he had a passion for Cree and wrote several poems in that language—he did not manage to establish a missionary school.

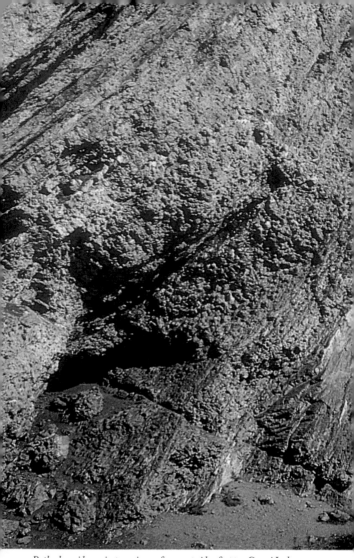

Path alongside ancient marine reef on west side of upper Grassi Lake.

9-Grassi Lakes

Difficulty: Easy to moderate
Distance: 1.6 km (0.99 mi)
Ascent Time: 40 minutes
Height Gain: 244 m (800 ft)
Elevation: 1670 m (5478 ft)
Topo Map: Canmore 82 O/3

Access: Take the turnoff to the Grassi Lakes, 1 km (0.62 mi) south of the Canmore Nordic Centre, on the Smith-Dorrien/ Spray Trail (Highway 742). The trailhead is located in the parking lot.

ocated close to the town of Canmore, Grassi Lakes is a place of exquisite beauty hidden from view in a narrow gorge flanked by sheer walls. Whether you have a leisurely half-day hike with a picnic in mind, a trip to the picto-graphs, or a rock climb on an ancient marine reef, Grassi Lakes has something to offer everyone. It is an excellent educational outing for the entire family and therefore can be very busy. The well-trodden trail to the turquoise lakes, which are suspended in

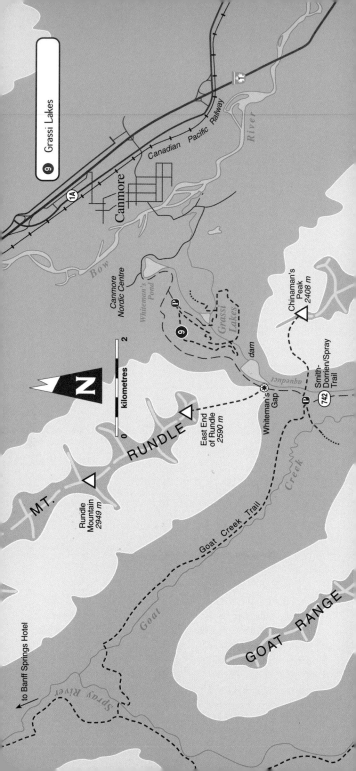

9 Grassi Lakes

Canadian Pacific Railway

Bow

River

1A

Canmore

Canmore
Nordic Centre

Whiteman's
Pond

P

9

Grassi
Lakes

dam

aqueduct

Chinaman's
Peak
2408 m

Smith-
Dorrien/Spray
Trail

742

P

Whiteman's
Gap

MT.

RUNDLE

East End
of Rundle
2590 m

Rundle
Mountain
2949 m

N

kilometres

0   2

Goat Creek Trail

Creek

Goat

GOAT RANGE

Spray River

to Banff Springs Hotel

Upper Grassi Lake.

a dramatic col between the east end of Mt. Rundle and Chinaman's Peak, makes for a very scenic afternoon.

From the parking lot, the well-trodden trail climbs gently through an aspen and lodgepole pine forest towards Whitcman's Gap. In a short distance, it splits, making it possible for the hiker to take a circuit route. The path to the left is more varied and climbs steeply towards a magnificent, 100-m (328-ft) waterfall that flows through the gorge from the lakes above. Log benches with interpretive signs provide interesting rest spots along the way. The trail follows the cliff edge, and twists uphill to climb the impressive rock staircase built by Lawrence Grassi, which leads to the azure lakes beyond.

Traverse left above the cliffs. Cross the bridge over Grassi Creek before merging with the TransAlta service road that leads to lower Grassi Lake. Considering the huge hydroelectric projects in the immediate vicinity that dammed and diverted waters from the Spray River through Whiteman's Gap and into the Bow Valley, Grassi Lakes were miraculously left in their natural state.

These two glittering jewels, which appear to be suspended in a dramatic canyon between the east end of Mt. Rundle and Chinaman's Peak, are remarkable for their colour and spectacular views of Canmore and the Bow Valley below. The transparent water reveals blooms of brown algae, resulting from the glacial water that seeps from the bedrock above. From the shore, the underwater coating of mud, brown slime and chartreuse fuzz resembles an abstract painting.

I dove into the lower lake one hot summer day and within seconds was out, gasping for air, thinking my heart had stopped, because the water was so cold. The water is also unbelievably still, and so clear that it is difficult to distinguish the adjacent, towering ancient reef from its reflection off the lake.

A gravel path with interpretive signs and wooden benches follows the shoreline of these pools, offering many opportunities to rest. You can explore the area from either direction. Apparently, the

Lawrence Grassi was a local miner and trail-builder, who was famous for his meticulous trails and superb craftsmanship here and in other locations in the Canadian Rockies, especially in the Lake O'Hara area. Lawrence Grassi and his friend Louis Joseph Kamenka built the trail to Grassi Lakes during a strike in the Canmore mines. The trail features trademark details, like a steep staircase made of Rundle rock, alongside the cascading waterfall that plummets from the lakes above. Originally named Twin Lakes, the lakes were renamed in Grassi's honour in 1938. Grassi died at the age of 90 in 1980.

only aquatic songbird in North America—the American dipper—lives here, feeding on larvae and nesting in the nearby rocks.

On the west side of upper Grassi Lake looms 270-m (886-ft) walls of Devonian tropical reef encrusted with fossils and coral-like sponges. The coarsely textured seabed, which dates back 370 million years to the Frasnian stage of the upper-Devonian period, is of great significance to the geologists who have done extensive research on it. The reef is fascinating to explore, and three shallow caves make an ideal lunch spot if it's raining.

It is possible to scramble upwards through the narrow canyon, maneuvering along logs and over gigantic boulders to explore more caves, scramble the Palliser dolostone cliffs, rock climb, or hunt for pictographs. Grassi Lakes is said to be a sacred site of the Stoney Indian band. Arrowheads dating back 8000 years have been found in the area. To see the rock paintings, climb up the badly eroded slope into the canyon above. The main image is on the large boulder directly ahead. The dolostone caves are said to have sheltered natives as recently as the 1700s. This steep route through the narrow gorge was once the old pack trail through Whiteman's Gap before the Smith Dorrien/Spray Trail was built. If you follow the trail to the top of the canyon, it ends at the Smith-Dorrien/Spray Trail (Highway 742) and Spray Reservoir.

American Dipper

It is also possible to descend to the Grassi Lakes from above, although this approach is so popular with rock climbers that it is often difficult to park. The rock walls are literally crawling with sport climbers, and some days it is so busy you could be on Banff Avenue.

To descend, retrace your steps to lower Grassi Lake and either continue down the path you ascended, or take the wide, grassy Trans Alta service road to the left back to the parking lot.

For hundreds of millions of years, continental plates under the earth's surface have been drifting, a continuously unfolding tectonic drama. Two hundred million years ago, the super-continent Pangaea began to break apart. The portion that is now known as North America reversed its motion and began the westward drift that eventually separated South America from the coast of Africa. The Rocky Mountain Trench is where the western edge of Pangaea was—on the west side of the Canadian Rockies. British Columbia was part of a vast ocean.

Sixty-five million years ago, the western edge of this ancient continent collided with the reef-like land off the western shore with such pressure that flat sea beds were pushed to the roof of the world, a process that initiated the building of the Canadian Rockies. (The plates are still continuing to drift.) At the same time harsh weather has eroded the peaks near Banff by approximately 2500 m (8200 ft) since their upthrust. The memory of ancient times is preserved in the twisted and folded rocks of the Canadian Rockies, and evidence of this geological history can be seen at Grassi Lakes, where an ancient marine reef has been thrust into a vertical wall.

On the northwest side of upper Grassi Lake is a porous wall that looks like something from the movie *Jurassic Park*. It turns out that it is even older. This Devonian reef is an inverted tropical seabed dating to the Frasnian stage of the upper-Devonian period during Paleozoic times, approximately 370 million years ago. This ancient marine reef is so old that it was already here 260 million years before the Laramide Orogeny—the term when the continental plates collided and created the upthrust of the Rockies. The section exposed at Grassi Lakes consists of fossils, or coral-like sponges, called stromatoporoids, which grew in a tropical climate, similar to the one Caribbean corals inhabit today. They sit on Cambrian rock that is over 500 million years old. Hikers can touch the rough, porous surface—rock climbers love its mottled face—and explore the numerous dolostone caves, which are a more recent feature (developed in the past few million years).

Numerous primitive reefs are buried throughout the Canadian Rockies—in fact, the minerals in a limestone massif are made from the calcium carbonate skeletons of corals. A Permian seabed exists on the banks of the Bow River near Bow Falls in Banff, but few are as accessible as the Devonian reef at Grassi Lakes. Whatever period the rocks are from, geologists can read the structure and composition of the mountains like a map. Evidence of most geological time periods exist in the sedimentary rocks around Banff, which all contain mineral deposits dating millions of years prior to the formation of the mountains.

Upper Grassi Lake looking towards Canmore and the Fairholme Range.

2
Best Dayhikes near the Town of Banff

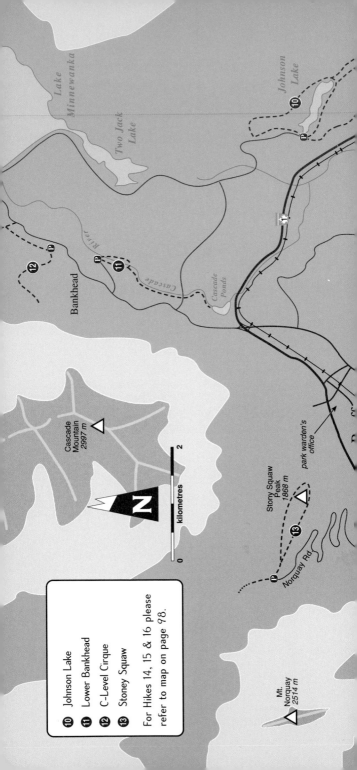

Lake Minnewanka

Johnson Lake

10

Two Jack Lake

Cascade River

12

12

11

Bankhead

Cascade Ponds

✈

Cascade Mountain
2997 m

▲

N

0   1   2
kilometres

Stony Squaw Peak
1868 m

▲

park warden's office

13

Norquay Rd.

Mt. Norquay
2514 m

▲

10 Johnson Lake

11 Lower Bankhead

12 C-Level Cirque

13 Stoney Squaw

For Hikes 14, 15 & 16 please refer to map on page 98.

The Banff area has a variety of interesting shorter hikes and activities to explore. (Looking west from Tunnel Mountain up the Bow Valley.)

10 – Johnson Lake

Difficulty: Easy
Distance: 2.4-km (1.5-mi) circuit
Time: 45 minutes
Elevation Gain: 10 m (33 ft)
Access. Follow Banff Avenue east. Pass under the TransCanada Highway onto Lake Minnewanka Road. In 1.2 km (0.75 mi) from the highway, turn right towards Johnson and Two Jack lakes. After a further 3.3 km (2 mi), turn right and follow the road to its end at Johnson Lake.

Johnson Lake is a popular picnic and swimming spot with Banff locals, because this artificial reservoir has much warmer water than the surrounding glacier-fed lakes. There are a variety of possible routes: an easy, 2.4-km (1.5-mi) loop that circles the lake, the slightly longer Anthracite Trail, which is 4.2 km (2.6 mi), as well as ski trails that offer good mountain bike terrain.

The lakeshore loop features great views and opportunities to see wildlife—elk, deer, sheep, muskrats, beavers, waterfowl and raptors. The sunny slopes on the north side are especially good for wildflowers. There are numerous Douglas fir trees—one of which is the oldest in the area at 700 years of age. The loop trail crosses the causeway at the far end of the lake, and follows a power line to a second lakeshore picnic site.

The Anthracite Trail loop begins on the footbridge at the west end of Johnson Lake. The crushed coal path descends into a gully, over coal tailing piles, through grassy meadows that were once the site of the coal mining town of Anthracite, and beneath the towering Anthracite hoodoo formations. The path then doubles back on the cliffs above the hoodoos to finish where you started at the first Johnson Lake picnic area.

Lake Minnewanka from C-Level Cirque.

11–Lower Bankhead

Difficulty: Easy
Distance: 1.1-km (0.68-mi) loop
Time: 45 minutes
Elevation Gain: 10 m (33 ft)
Access: Follow Banff Avenue east of town until you reach the TransCanada Highway. Keep going straight on the Lake Minnewanka Road to a parking area at 3.3 km (2 mi) on the right side of the road.

This easy, 1.1-km (0.68-mi) loop to the Bankhead interpretive exhibit is interesting for history buffs—it explores a coal mining town that flourished in the early 1900s. The trail takes you past the ruins of the industrial complex, a mining train and slag heaps. Named after a Scottish town, the Bankhead mine was created to supply the CPR's coal needs. It operated successfully from 1903–22 until a decade-long economic slump and an eight-month strike forced the mine to close. The vibrant community of mostly Chinese workers turned into a ghost town.

A brochure available at the trailhead provides a brief history of the town. A 2.5-km (1.6-mi) extension to the interpretive trail follows the defunct Bankhead railway south to Cascade Ponds, which is a great place to spend a lazy summer afternoon. The picnic site is equipped with tables, fire pits, shelters and a man-made pond excellent for swimming.

12-C-Level Cirque

Difficulty: Easy to Moderate
Distance: 3.9 km (2.4 mi)
Return Time: 2 hrs
Elevation Gain: 430 m (1410 ft)
Access: Follow Banff Avenue east of town until you reach the TransCanada Highway. Keep straight ahead on the Lake Minnewanka Road for 3.7 km (2.3 mi), then turn left into the Upper Bankhead picnic area.

Hikers who wish to explore the Bankhead area further should take this steep hike that passes two abandoned mines. 'C-Level Cirque' refers to the level of the coal seam that was mined at Bankhead. It is located beneath the impressive cliffs and talus slopes on the east face of Cascade Mountain. The trail passes a huge coal tailings pile, and has excellent views of Lake Minnewanka, the Fairholme Range, Mt. Rundle, Cascade Mountain and the Bow Valley. Between the mine and the entrance to the cirque, the trail continues uphill and cuts through several coal seams, before entering a dense forest that leads to the cirque. A faint path heads north along the eastern edge of the cirque to a larch-covered knoll, which offers more spectacular views. Wildlife, especially bighorn sheep, are often seen on this hike, as is the exotic glacier lily in spring.

A montane forest with Douglas fir.

13–Stoney Squaw

Difficulty: Easy to Moderate
Distance: 2.2 km (1.4 mi)
Return Time: 1.5 hrs
Elevation Gain: 230 m (754 ft)
Access: Follow Mt. Norquay
Road north across the
TransCanada Highway
interchange, and continue
to the main parking lot at the
Mt. Norquay ski resort 6 km
(3.7 mi) from Banff. The trail
starts near the S.E. corner.

The Stoney Squaw trail climbs at a moderate grade through a thick forest to the summit of Stoney Squaw, a low peak across from Mt. Norquay. At 1868 m (6127 ft), Stoney Squaw is higher than Tunnel Mountain, and has excellent panoramic views of the Banff townsite, Bow Valley, Fairholme Range, Cascade Mountain and Mt. Rundle. The rounded nubs of both Tunnel Mountain and Stoney Squaw were covered in ice during the Wisconsin ice age. Some of the rocks at the trail's end contain fossils and corals. If you want to, there is also a loop trail to hike; continue down the northern slope through a lovely subalpine forest carpeted with feather mosses to arrive back at the Mt. Norquay ski resort.

The trail to Sundance Canyon offers amazing views of Mt. Edith.

14-Sundance Canyon

Difficulty: Easy
Distance: 3.8 km (2.4 mi)
Ascent Time: 1 hr
Elevation Gain: 75 m (246 ft)
Access: Follow Banff Avenue south across the Bow River bridge, and turn right at the lights onto Cave Avenue. Follow Cave Avenue to its end at the Cave & Basin parking lot. The trailhead to Sundance Canyon is located at the right of the Cave & Basin facility.

Sundance Canyon is a very popular picnic site. After an initially hectic start, during which you share the wheelchair-accessible path with cyclists, rollerbladers, joggers and horses, the easy, 3.8-km (2.4-mi) path eventually winds along the Bow River to a canyon that has been eroded into the bedrock. There is some great scenery and, at the 2-km (1.2-mi) mark, a rest spot with benches, which offers dramatic views of the overthrust mountain, Mt. Edith. The junction at 2.6 km (1.6 mi) from the trailhead intersects with trails leading up the west slope of Sulphur Mountain and to Healy Creek. Keep straight ahead for the Sundance Canyon picnic area and the footpath, which explores the canyon and a series of waterfalls. There is a 2.1-km (1.3-mi) loop extension with glimpses of the Sawback Range before the trail descends back to the picnic area.

View from Bow Falls of the Banff Springs Hotel.

15-Bow Falls

Difficulty: Easy
Distance: 2.3 km (1.4 mi)
Time: 1 hr
Elevation Gain: 10 m (33 ft)
Access: From downtown Banff, cross the Bow River bridge and turn right onto Spray Avenue. After 0.8 km (0.5 mi), turn left on Rundle Avenue and follow it to the Bow Falls parking lot.

Bow Falls can be seen from different viewpoints. It is possible to drive or walk there on either side of the Bow River from the Banff townsite. The paved, wheelchair-accessible pathway begins at the north end of Bow Avenue on Echo Creek, near the canoe rental operation, north of Wolf Street, and continues past Central Park to the Bow River bridge. From the bridge, trails continue on either side of the river. Continuing on the north side trail takes you along the riverbank and up Tunnel Mountain Drive to a path that leads to a parking lot overlooking the falls. From here, take the trail to the right. It descends to Bow Falls. (The trail to the left goes to the Bow River Hoodoos.) Nearby is a sandy beach on the Bow River.

The route south of the bridge takes you along a trail to Glen Avenue, which veers to the right, before returning shortly to the river path. Here, you can either climb the first set of stairs to follow along the cliff of the Bow River, or bypass them, take a gravel trail to the right, and then climb a second set of stairs leading to the riverbank cliff. From the cliff, there are great views of the rapids before the water cascades over the 10-m (33-ft) cliffs. Descend the stairs to see the famous view of the Bow Falls from the parking lot below the Banff Springs Hotel.

16-Spray River Loop

Difficulty: Easy
Distance: 13-km (8-mi) circuit
Time: 4–6 hrs
Elevation Gain: 200 m (656 ft)
Access: Begin this loop either
from the Banff Springs Hotel golf
course parking lot at Bow Falls or
from the Banff Springs Hotel
parking lot, to the right of the
statue of Cornelius Van Horne.

The Spray River Loop is an easy and popular hike that explores the Spray River. This area is prime wildlife terrain. Wolves and grizzly bears have been sighted here, as well as the more usual elk, bighorn sheep and mountain goats. Begin at the golf course across the Spray River bridge and watch for a hiker sign, indicating the Spray River East Road. This wide hiker/horse trail exits the golf course and climbs steeply through the montane forest before levelling off into more undulating terrain a few hundred metres later. At 1.6 km (1 mi) the Rundle trail branches left. Keep straight ahead. At 2.1 km (1.3 mi) the Spray River East Road emerges from the forest along open bluffs high above the Spray River. There are excellent views of the Banff Springs Hotel. The trail then re-enters the forest, passing a campground and crossing a footbridge, to arrive at the picnic area and junction with the Spray River West Road and Goat Creek Trail to Canmore.

This area is an excellent place to stop for lunch, either at the picnic tables or in a more private spot along the river. For the return trip on the west side of the river, take the Spray River West Road, which descends into the valley, past the Canadian Youth Hostel, to the Spray River West Road access gate. From here, you can either stay on the trail to arrive at the Banff Springs Hotel parking lot, or make your way back to Bow Falls by any number of routes. One trail branches off

Mountain Goat

to the right about 0.5 km (0.3 mi) before the Banff Springs Hotel, then winds down to the Spray River, crosses a footbridge, and continues along the river to the golf course at Bow Falls.

3
Best Dayhikes in the Town of Banff

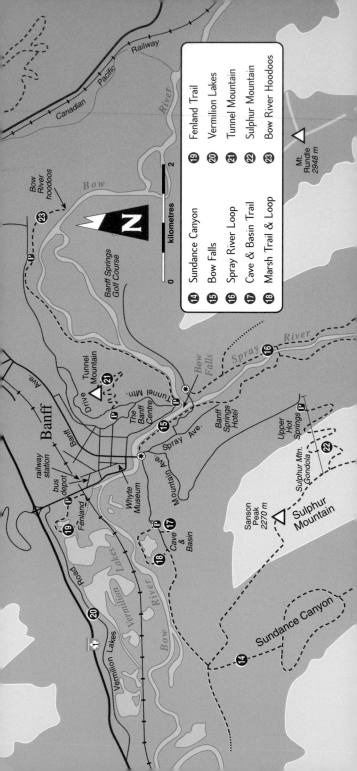

⑲	Fenland Trail	⑭	Sundance Canyon
⑳	Vermilion Lakes	⑮	Bow Falls
㉑	Tunnel Mountain	⑯	Spray River Loop
㉒	Sulphur Mountain	⑰	Cave & Basin Trail
㉓	Bow River Hoodoos	⑱	Marsh Trail & Loop

Mt. Rundle
2948 m

N

0 kilometres 2

Bow River hoodoos

Canadian Pacific Railway

River

Bow

㉓

Banff Springs Golf Course

Spray River

⑯

Bow Falls

Tunnel Mountain

㉑

Tunnel Mtn.

The Banff Centre

⑮

Banff Springs Hotel

Upper Hot Springs

Sulphur Mtn. Gondola

㉒

Banff Ave.

Banff

Tunnel Mtn. Drive

railway station

bus depot

Fenland

⑲

Fenland

Whyte Museum

Spray Ave.

Mountain Ave.

Sanson Peak
2270 m

Sulphur Mountain

⑰

Cave & Basin

⑱

Vermilion Lakes

⑳

Vermilion Lakes Road

Bow River

Sundance Canyon

⑭

Mt. Rundle (north face) with Vermilion Lakes in foreground.

Vermilion Wetlands

Not everyone wants to climb a mountain. Many people choose to investigate amphibians in a montane marsh, hunt for exotic orchids and other aquatic bog life, or watch a belted kingfisher dive for an early morning snack—all at a lower altitude. Visitors will be happy to know that there is plenty of terrain to explore close to Banff in an area known as the Vermilion wetlands, which encompasses three lakes, two creeks and numerous marshes, bogs and fens. The Vermilion wetlands used to be the home of an ancient lake dating back 11,000 years ago to when the glacial ice receded.

The warm mineral water from the hot springs, which flows down the lower slopes of Sulphur Mountain, makes this area of special interest. The water has such a moderating effect on the climate that the Vermilion wetlands don't freeze during harsh winter months. The local environment is changed so drastically that certain plants remain green throughout the year, and normally migratory birds like the killdeer, mallard duck, snipe and American robin stay the winter. The marshes, swamps and fens that make up the Vermilion wetlands are home to a startling number of exotic plant, fish, bird and reptile species unique to the Banff area. Visitors can explore this unusual habitat on the Marsh Trail & Loop, the Cave & Basin Discovery Trail, the Fenland Trail or at Vermilion Lakes. All locations are a naturalist's dream, and offer some of the best birding in the Canadian Rockies.

The Cave & Basin Discovery Trail and the Marsh Trail & Loop are located in the Vermilion wetlands.

17-Cave & Basin Discovery Trail

18-Marsh Trail & Loop

Difficulty: Easy interpretive trails; wheelchair accessible
Distance: 0.8–2.7 km (0.5–1.8 mi)
Time: 20 minutes (both trails)
Elevation Gain: 15 m (49 ft)
Access: Follow Banff Avenue south across the Bow River bridge, turn right at the lights, and follow Cave Avenue to its end at the Cave & Basin parking lot. Take the paved pedestrian path to the Cave & Basin facility. Phone number: (403) 762-1557.

The Cave & Basin National Historic Site is open daily, June to Labour Day, 9 a.m.–6 p.m., and 9:30 a.m.–5 p.m. throughout the rest of the year. Visitors can feel the warm waters and see the original hot spring in the cave. The facility has an exhibition hall and a 15-minute, award-winning slide presentation about how the chance discovery of the hot springs led to the foundation of the national parks system. The complex also has picnic tables, a licensed tea room, a gift shop and washrooms. It is no longer possible to swim at the Cave & Basin. Instead, check out the outdoor soaking pool at the Upper Hot Springs, which is the hottest of the five springs on Sulphur Mountain and was renovated in 1996. Call (403) 762-1515 for information.

The Discovery Trail begins up the stone stairs to the left of the Cave & Basin. A wooden boardwalk

Interpretive signs on the Discovery Trail point out highlights of the wetlands and Cave & Basin.

takes visitors to an opening above the sulphur cave, where the hot springs were discovered, and to a spring flowing out of the hillside. There are interpretive signs along the trail explaining the geological implications and historical relevance of the springs to Banff National Park and platforms to view the tropical flora and fauna of the wetlands. Benches along the trail allow you to relax and enjoy the views.

The Marsh Trail and Marsh Loop are to the right of the main Cave & Basin building. The 10-minute boardwalk loop leads along the edge of the unique wetland, where it is possible to view wildlife and exotic plants. There are benches and interpretive signs along the way. On the marsh itself is a floating boardwalk and bird blind for photographers and bird watchers. Native fish such as minnows and sticklebacks can be seen darting about in the warm waters, hiding in the profusion of underwater plants, white and blue-green algae and bright pink bacteria. Tropical fish have been introduced to this environment from indoor aquariums, and have done so well that they threaten the eight native species of fish. In fact, the Banff longnose dace was declared extinct in 1991, a casualty of human tampering in the ecosystem.

If you want to explore the wetlands further, take the 2.7-

Warm waters on Discovery Trail.

km (1.7-mi) extension to the Marsh Trail. It leads visitors through the marshes below the Cave & Basin and along Echo Creek, a creek that flows from First Vermilion Lakes and merges with Forty Mile Creek. It provides an opportunity to investigate the marsh area in detail—it is possible to see exotic orchids and primroses, algae blooms in still ponds, sphagnum mosses and bog plants such as bog cranberry, crowberry, Labrador tea and swamp laurel. You may also see a swimming muskrat or a beaver lodge. This path crosses a horse trail, which leads to Sundance Canyon, so you may have to step aside to let a trail ride pass.

Common Muskrat

Bank erosion in Fenland.

19-Fenland Trail

Difficulty: Easy; wheelchair accessible
Distance: 1.5-km (0.93-mi) loop
Time: 30 minutes
Elevation Gain: Negligible
Access: The Fenland or Forty Mile Creek picnic area is 400 m (1312 ft) north of the CPR track on the west side of the Mt. Norquay Road.

The Fenland is a pleasant place for a picnic, an afternoon canoe trip, or a stroll through an unusual ecosystem in the mountains. This short loop trail can be easily reached on foot from the Banff townsite, and is located at the rear of the Forty Mile Creek picnic area. Interpretive brochures are stocked at a dispenser. Cross the footbridge and continue straight ahead at the T-junction for the self-guided nature walk. The clockwise direction allows you to visit 10 interpretive stops in sequence. The path to the left leads away from the fen and follows the creek back to Mt. Norquay Road in 100 m (328 ft).

Along this trail you are witnessing how the marsh environment is transformed into a montane forest—a process called succession. A wetland is an area where the water table is above or at the same level as the soil. There are different classes of wetlands: bogs, fens, swamps and marshes. A fen is drier than a marsh, but wetter than a bog or swamp. At various points along the trail, hikers can see open swamps, areas where beavers have been at work, and evidence of spring floods. These floods speed up the last stage of fenland succession by washing silt and dead plants into the fen, changing the acidity of the soil, and creating more habitat for vegetation to grow.

Sedges, grasses, aquatics, ferns, horsetails and mosses make this mineral-rich fenland a naturalist's paradise. The shady level path travels along Forty Mile Creek and through an ancient white spruce forest, one of the oldest in the Banff vicinity; the wetlands provide a natural barrier against fires. Fallen trees lie submerged in the clear waters, sometimes toppled by beavers or by spring runoff, which submerges the banks and floods the placid waters. Canals leading to mounds of sticks and mud provide safe shelter from coyotes and bears for aquatic rodents. Willow, aspen and red osier dogwood are important food sources for

the ungulates—deer, elk and moose—that frequent the area. Alpine bearberry is a delicacy with bears. Claw marks left by black bears are noticeable on the bark of trembling aspen trees.

At the edge of the fen are tiny, pink primroses, round-leafed orchids, shooting stars and butterworts. Numerous moisture-loving plants grow in the thick, black mud. It is a good place to look for clusters of white-bog orchids, purple-bog violets or pink little elephants. Further into the fen, the ground gets spongy and provides a good climate for sedges, rushes, horsetails and cotton grasses. In places where the water is still, the ground is carpeted with bright green feather mosses.

Forty Mile Creek and Echo Creek create a natural moat, which protects the interior of the fen from predators. During the elk calving season in June, the trail is usually closed because mothers use the area to raise their young. These adult animals can be extremely dangerous, and will stand on their hind legs to pummel victims with their razor-sharp hooves, causing serious bodily harm. Bull elk are just as aggressive in fall when they often attack people during the rut. So, if the trails are closed, keep out!

West side of Rundle from the Vermilion Lakes.

20-Vermilion Lakes

Difficulty: Easy
Distance: 4.3 km (2.7 mi)
Time: 1–1.5 hrs
Elevation Gain: 10 m (33 ft)
Access: The junction of
Vermilion Lakes Drive and Mt.
Norquay Road, approximately
700 m (2296 ft) north of the
CPR tracks on the west side of
the road.

The Vermilion Lakes is
within walking distance
of the Banff townsite,
and is an excellent location to
visit by foot, bike or vehicle.
Vermilion Lakes Drive meanders alongside the lakes and
offers classic views of Mt.
Rundle. At the end of the
drive is an old road that leads
through a white spruce forest
for 1 km (0.62 mi) to its end
at the TransCanada Highway.
There is a parking area with
washrooms at 3.7 km (2.3 mi)
between the second and third
lakes.

With the highway so
close, Vermilion Lakes is cer-

wildflowers, as well as exotic grasses growing in the lakes. Sedges, aquatics, ferns, horsetails and mosses make this area a botanist's gold mine. Archeologists have gathered evidence of human activity in this area dating back 11,000 years. Coyote, elk, moose, mule deer, mink, muskrat, beaver, black bear and, occasionally, wolves all frequent the area. The Fenland Trail and Vermilion Lakes are also two of the best birding locations in the Canadian Rockies. The mixture of forest, shrubs and marsh provides a home to an astounding variety of species.

Large raptors (red-tailed hawks, bald eagles, barred owls and ospreys), water birds (Canadian geese, grebes, common mergansers, mallards, green-winged teals and loons) and song birds (flycatchers, swallows, eastern kingbirds, common yellow throats, red-winged blackbirds, black-capped chickadees, varied thrushes, hairy woodpeckers, ruby-crowned kinglets and yellow-rumped warblers) can be spotted, as well as belted kingfishers, American dippers, hummingbirds and tundra swans.

Insects are as abundant as the bird population. Mosquitoes are voracious, so make sure to bring insect repellent.

tainly not a wilderness destination, although many people find serenity in the beautiful landscape and turquoise waters. It can make for a very relaxing afternoon away from downtown Banff. There are pullouts at each lake, and locals often sunbathe on the wooden boat docks, which provide a restful spot near the shore. Even more relaxing is a canoe trip on the lakes to Forty Mile Creek and Echo Creek.

The shoreline has many small paths to explore the aquatic region. There is an abundance of moisture-loving

Summit of Tunnel with Rundle in background.

Tunnel & Sulphur Mountains

For those visitors who want to climb a mountain peak but not leave the Banff townsite, both Tunnel and Sulphur mountains offer superb views of the area, are close by the town, and provide an alternative to shopping.

21-Tunnel Mountain

Difficulty: Easy to Moderate
Distance: 2.3 km (1.4 mi)
Ascent Time: 30 minutes
Elevation Gain: 305 m (1000 ft)
Elevation: 1690 m (5543 ft)
Access: The lower trailhead is located in the N.E. corner of the overflow parking lot for The Banff Centre on the east side of St. Julien Road, 350 m (1148 ft) south of Wolf Street. Look for the hiker sign. Another approach is from the upper parking lot on Tunnel Mountain Drive, south of the junction with Tunnel Mountain Road. It is a good alternative to those hikers who wish to avoid the steepest section of the trail.

For hikers with only a few hours to spare, the all-season hike up Tunnel Mountain is short and offers excellent views of the Banff townsite and Bow Corridor. Because of the easy access from downtown Banff and the relatively easy grade, this trail is probably hiked more than any other. The well-maintained path ascends the west side of Tunnel Mountain. It is steepest at the outset and switchbacks to a viewpoint at the upper trailhead. From here, the trail moderates to an easy incline, and winds through a thick forest of Douglas fir and lodgepole pine up to the summit. There are shady sections with scenic lookouts along the way that make for delightful hiking. As you gain elevation, there are impressive views of the Banff Springs Hotel and Sulphur Mountain, Mt. Norquay and the Vermilion wetlands towards Mt. Bourgeau. To the north, Cascade Mountain is the highest mountain peak in the area at 2998 m (9833 ft).

The path leads north along a ridge, and climbs gently to the summit on the east side of the mountain, which was once the site of the Tunnel Mountain fire lookout tower. The panoramic view is superb: great views to the southeast of the dramatic north ridge of Mt. Rundle, the Banff Springs Golf Course and Bow River valley to the eastern edge of the Fairholme Range near Exshaw. There is a great temptation to peer down over the many sheer cliffs to get better views of the Bow River. Do this with extreme caution, since people have fallen to their deaths here. Tunnel Mountain was once part of Rundle, until glacial ice eroded a chasm between them during the Wisconsin ice age.

In 1882, Major A.J. Rogers, a surveyor for the CPR, proposed that a tunnel be blasted through the mountain to make way for the railroad. Fortunately, another surveyor, Charles A. Shaw, found a less expensive route between Tunnel Mountain and Cascade Mountain. He commented, 'I cannot understand why they failed to investigate the valley to the west ... Rogers' location here was the most extraordinary blunder ever known in the way of engineering.' Tunnel Mountain is also a sacred mountain for the Stoney Natives who originally named it Sleeping Buffalo Mountain, because of its resemblance to a bison when viewed from the east.

Looking northwest towards the Vermilion wetlands from Sulphur Mountain.

22-Sulphur Mountain

Difficulty: Moderate to Strenuous
Distance: 5.5 km (3.4 mi)
Ascent Time: 2–2.5 hrs
Elevation Gain: 660 m (2165 ft)
Elevation: 2260 m (7415 ft)
Access: Follow Banff Avenue south, cross the Bow River bridge, and turn left onto Spray Avenue. Turn right onto Sulphur Mountain Drive, and follow it to the upper parking lot for the Upper Hot Springs. The trailhead is beside a steel gate, which is across the old access road in the N.W. corner of the parking lot at the bottom of the road leading to the pool.

While most tourists take the gondola up Sulphur Mountain, the hike to the top is a pleasant alternative. In mid-August when Banff Avenue is crowded with visitors, it is still possible to experience a sense of wilderness and solitude in the Banff townsite. The coolness of the montane and subalpine forests provides a refreshing break from the summer heat. Although the hike is strenuous, it is easy overall, because of the well-graded road to the top.

At the trailhead, follow a steep road that turns right

and then switchbacks left 100 m (328 ft) from the trailhead before its grade moderates. There is a waterfall at 2.2 km (1.4 mi), and the trail switchbacks to the right. At 2.6 km (1.6 mi), the trail up the west side of Sulphur Mountain, which splits off from the Sundance Canyon Trail, joins the path. At 2.7 km (1.7 mi) there is an old cabin that was used prior to the construction of the gondola in 1959. A tractor pulled tourists this far. The grade steepens and zigzags underneath the gondola for the next 3 km up to the summit ridge (5.4 km).

Once you arrive at the gondola station and teahouse located on the summit ridge, the illusion of being lost in the wilderness is shattered. Here, hundreds of tourists line up to experience the thrill of being on a mountain peak. Armed with cameras and video equipment, they jockey for position to record themselves in the spectacular setting. Well-designed boardwalks with interpretive signs (including panoramic illustrations corresponding to the mountain peaks beyond) lead visitors to the old weather station, which was

Looking southeast down the Goat Creek Valley.

used by Norman Sanson at the summit of Sanson Peak. This mountain is 400 m (1312 ft) from the trailhead.

Norman Sanson (1862–1949) climbed the trail weekly from 1903–31 to take meteorological readings. At age 70, Sanson was so fit he could still reach the summit in less than two hours. Occasionally, when it took him several hours to reach the top, he was forced to stay the night in the observatory because of harsh weather conditions. On July 1, 1931, Banff locals accompanied him to the top to honour him with a sunrise breakfast in celebration of his 1000th ascent. In 1945, the 83-year-old man climbed to the summit to observe a solar eclipse. Sanson was the first president of Skyline Trail Hikers and

Looking northeast from Sulphur Mountain over Tunnel Mountain and Bow River.

curator of the Banff Park Museum from 1896–1931.

Sulphur Mountain, at 2260 m (7413 ft) high, is one of the tallest peaks in the Banff area. Its sweeping views are spectacular and worth braving the crowds to see. It offers an excellent overview of the Banff Springs Hotel and golf course, Vermilion wetlands and the Sundance and Goat ranges as well as distant views down the Goat Creek valley. Tunnel and Rundle mountains are well within view, and so are notable peaks like Cascade, Norquay, Edith, Cory, Louis and Bourgeau.

It is possible to wander off the boardwalk and, for those who enjoy scrambling, there are many opportunities to do so on granite-like boulders on the less-crowded ridge to the south. For those visitors who don't want to hike back down the mountain, the gondola is free of charge for the ride down. Check hours of operation by calling (403) 762 2523.

The Bow River Hoodoos have been eroded into fantastic shapes by water, wind and snow.

23-Bow River Hoodoos

Difficulty: Easy to Moderate
Distance: 0.5-km (0.31-mi) interpretive walk or 5-km (3-mi) trail from Bow Falls
Time: 10 minutes; 2.5 hrs return
Elevation Gain: 5 m (16 ft)
Elevation: 1410 m (4625 ft)
Access: The trailhead for the interpretive walk is at the hoodoos parking lot on the south side of Tunnel Mountain Road, across from the Tunnel Mountain campground. The alternative Bow Falls route begins at the Bow Falls viewpoint on Tunnel Mountain Drive near The Banff Centre.

Perched on a steep hill guarding the Bow River are intriguing pilars of rock that resemble stone gods whose ancient bodies are gradually being reclaimed by the spirit world. Eroded for centuries by wind and water, these mute witnesses to history have stood in silence while the Wisconsin ice age slid away. Did they watch the tongue of a slowly advancing glacier carve Tunnel Mountain from the side of Rundle, making room for a river of ice? Did they see the first human inhabitants journey along the Bow River valley some 11,000 years ago? The hoodoos saw it all. But chances are they won't

The Bow River Hoodoos walk provides great views of Mt. Rundle.

awaken to tell their stories. As time erodes their bodies, so, too, will history be eroded.

Today, these resistant spires are as magical to geomorphologists and geologists as they were to the Stoney Natives. By examining the hoodoos' composition, we understand history perhaps better than if they could speak. Hoodoos were formed at the end of the Wisconsin ice age, from till left behind by the glacial advance that extended beyond Banff, carving a U-shaped valley down the Bow Corridor. When the glaciers receded and the ice melted, the Bow River eroded into the till, or ground moraine, to form steep banks.

Wind, rain and spring runoff eroded furrows into the banks. These furrows continually deepened to produce these enigmatic shapes.

Hoodoos are made of glacial till—mud and stones—cemented together by the calcium carbonate (the main compound when making cement) that existed in the original limestone and dolomite rocks. Under the influence of precipitation, the hoodoos developed into rocklike pillars of tillite. The cap rocks, which protected hoodoos from being washed away, have long since vanished, so weather will eventually erode these hoodoos to extinction.

Without their cap rocks, the hoodoos will eventually collapse from weather erosion.

To view them from above, take the short stroll along the asphalt path, which leads to three viewpoints with interpretive signs that explain the hoodoos' geomorphic significance. If you want a closer look, follow one of the many steep paths eroded into the open slope to the base of the hoodoos.

Alternatively, you may want to extend the outing by 5 km (3 mi) and begin the hike at the Bow Falls parking lot on Tunnel Mountain Drive. Take the stairs descending to the river where the trail divides. The path to the right has better views of the Fairholme Range and the imposing north face of Rundle than the path to the left. The right path winds through a Douglas fir forest and maneuvers around the south cliffs of Tunnel Mountain. In a short distance, either climb another set of stairs or, if the river is low, walk along the riverbank. When the routes rejoin, you will go through a meadow before climbing up to Tunnel Mountain Road and the official asphalt path to the hoodoos' viewing platforms and interpretive displays.

About the Author

Heather Elton lives in Calgary, where she works as a free-lance editor, writer and photographer. She has founded two award-winning Canadian art magazines, *Last Issue* and *Dance Connection*. Her photographs have appeared in *Saturday Night*, *Western Living*, *Explore*, *Flare* and *West* magazines. She is an avid hiker and telemark skier, and has been touring through the Canadian Rockies since 1970. Her travels have taken her throughout Western Europe and Eastern Europe, Hong Kong, Hawaii, Costa Rica, Venezuela and along the Maya Route through Mexico, Belize and Guatemala.

Index

ANIMAL TRACKS OF THE ROCKIES

Learn the track shape, stride pattern, travel habits and other fascinating facts about the animals in the Rocky Mountains. Identify any track from shrew to grizzly bear in snow, sand or mud. Whether you're an urban explorer or a backwoods bushwacker, this pocket guide will provide many hours of outdoor education and entertainment all year-round!

ISBN 1-55105-089-7
160 pages • softcover
b & w illustrations • 4.25" x 5.75"
$7.95 CDN $5.95 US

BIRDS OF THE ROCKY MOUNTAINS

This lavishly illustrated guide contains more than 300 species of common and interesting birds whose ranges encompass the Rockies from Alberta and British Columbia south through Montana, Idaho, Wyoming, Utah, Colorado and New Mexico.

ISBN 1-55105-091-9
352 pages • softcover
color illustrations • 5.5" x 8.5"
$24.95 CDN $19.95 US

PLANTS OF THE ROCKY MOUNTAINS

The Rocky Mountains encompass many plant communities, including alpine tundra, majestic Douglas-fir forests, wildflower meadows and dry grassy sites. This handy guide describes common species in the Rocky Mountains from Alberta and British Columbia through to Colorado. The detailed species descriptions are combined with precise drawings and excellent color photographs.

ISBN 1-55105-088-9
384 pages • softcover
color illustrations • 5.5" x 8.5"
$19.95 US $24.95 CDN

Lone Pine Publishing

Phone Toll-Free
1-800-661-9017

Fax Toll-Free
1-800-424-7173